shared confinement

HEALING OPTIONS FOR YOU & THE AGORAPHOBIC IN YOUR LIFE

ROBERT C. CHOPE, PH.D.

New Harbinger Publications, Inc.

Distributed in the U.S.A. by Publishers Group West; in Canada by Raincoast Books; in Great Britain by Airlift Book Company, Ltd.; in South Africa by Real Books, Ltd.; in Australia by Boobook; and in New Zealand by Tandem Press.

Copyright © 2001 by Robert C. Chope
New Harbinger Publications, Inc.
5674 Shattuck Avenue
Oakland, CA 94609

Cover design © by Lightbourne Images
Edited by Clancy Drake
Text design by Tracy Powell-Carlson

Library of Congress Card Catalogue Number: 01-132258
ISBN 1-57224-266-3 Paperback

New Harbinger Publications' Web site address: www.newharbinger.com

03   02   01

10   9   8   7   6   5   4   3   2   1

First printing

To Roberta Ann Johnson: confidante, teacher, partner, friend

Contents

Preface

This book is my modest attempt to acknowledge scores of unsung heroes who provide calming interventions and caregiving services to their agoraphobic companions and loved ones. As a psychologist, I get paid to help out; family members and companions don't. But they deserve platinum medallions, quite clearly more than I do.

The book is intended as a helpful guide for people who care for an agoraphobe. You may prefer to read it all the way through, or you may wish to peruse chapters dealing with specific issues. No matter. Each chapter gives you an opportunity to apply different material and suggestions to your particular circumstances.

As you undoubtedly know, agoraphobia is a tricky disorder, lacking a single well-defined treatment protocol. And you know how confounding life can be as a caregiver to an agoraphobe. It may be evident that your companion's problems have piled a few difficulties upon you. Perhaps you experience loss of sleep, major appetite swings, concentration problems, or just frustration. You may be lonely, feeling just as isolated from friends as your agoraphobe is. This book will help you dig out from some of the misfortune you feel by providing concrete advice for you, your family, and your companion.

Many people have assisted me with this project. The staff at New Harbinger Publications has been steadfastly supportive from the onset, as always. Former acquisitions editor Kristen Beck encouraged me to prepare the original proposal for the book, and publisher

Matt McKay further embraced the idea. Acquisitions editor Catharine Sutker reviewed and approved my revised proposal, editorial manager Heather Garnos Mitchener served as midpoint editor, and Clancy Drake was copy editor. Other New Harbinger staff who gave time and assistance include lead publicist Kasey Pfaff, and art director Amy Shoup. The Office of Public Affairs at San Francisco State University, which has been instrumental in reviewing, promoting, and publicizing my written work and community contributions for years, also deserves special acknowledgment. Thanks also to my students in the Department of Counseling at San Francisco State University for the class periods we devoted to discussing the many clinical issues of caregiving.

As with all of my professional projects, my colleague and partner, Roberta Ann Johnson, Ph.D., of the University of San Francisco, kept me focused. While she is certainly the safest critic I've ever had, she is also the most forthright. For her assistance and love, I'm eternally grateful. My children, Jeff and Luisa, enthusiastically endorsed my work and throughout the project asked for periodic updates.

Finally, I would like to thank the caregivers who motivated me to write about their stories. I hardly know most of you, though I know your agoraphobic companions quite well. But it was through your words in your phone calls, notes, and e-mails that I was able to become keenly aware of your plight. I hope this book does service to your concerns.

Introduction

In my career as a counselor over the last quarter century, I've treated people with all sorts of fear, panic, and anxiety disorders. In fact, I've had some extraordinary experiences attending to each of the anxiety disorders listed in the *Diagnostic and Statistical Manual of Mental Disorders* (fourth edition, text revision) (hereafter referred to as the DSM-IV-TR): acute stress disorder, agoraphobia, generalized anxiety disorder, obsessive-compulsive disorder, post-traumatic stress disorder, specific (formerly "simple") phobias, social phobia, and some that are as yet "not otherwise specified." This range of experience wouldn't be astounding except that none of it occurred in a hospital-based, clinical psychology practice.

The individuals I cared for received services at the Career and Personal Development Institute in San Francisco, a facility dedicated primarily to planning career and life transitions. The constellation of menacing anxiety disorders I encountered emerged from the narratives of individuals who were going about the business of making life decisions and dealing with the accompanying changes. For many, a crisis or a major life change provoked symptoms of phobias that became increasingly hard-core and challenging to vanquish.

Change Is Tough

What people in life transitions discover is that change of any kind is emotionally demanding. It's thoroughly unpredictable and stressful, and it calls for adaptability and flexibility. People engaged in everyday changes are often touched by fear and anxiety related to the risks they're taking.

As a reader of this book you may have special concerns. You may be interested in learning about fresh new ways to relate to and cope with a loved one's difficulties. Or you may have your own rapidly cascading fears about what's going to change in your life as you assume the role of primary caregiver for someone you're close to. Whatever your concerns, this book will provide you with helpful information and a new perspective on caring for an agoraphobe.

Anxiety: America's Premier Mental Health Problem

M. E. Lerner (2000) reported that anxiety is America's number one mental health problem. It costs us more than $42 billion per year. That sounds like a lot of money, but if work-related productivity loss and absence are counted, as well as the costs of psychotherapy, prescription drugs, and other forms of treatment, then it's a pretty good estimate. Moreover, the prevalence of anxiety is increasing, and many of my colleagues believe, as I do, that the increase is due to the head-spinning amount of uncertainty in our lives.

Uncertainty is everywhere. There's doubt about the work world even in times of relative economic prosperity. I suppose that's why I, as someone who works in the area of career development, have so much exposure to the family of anxiety disorders. But the rapidly escalating costs of energy and housing are also customary causes of worry as are the unpredictable stock markets and the frequency of school violence. The streets of any city seem to be filled with phalanxes of people who have a bleary-eyed, worried look.

Of the roughly 23 million people who suffer from some sort of anxiety disorder, half are phobics. They've often tried to handle their issues by staying away from circumstances that make them feel uneasy, but many still feel like they're going out of their minds. In fact, retreating from the causes of anxiety, fear, phobias, and general worry is probably the least effective strategy. The most powerful and fruitful approach is to deal with these feelings head on using some form of real-life immersion coupled with strategies to enhance relaxation and desensitization. You'll learn about such strategies in this book.

Agoraphobia

The most complex and intriguing of the anxiety disorders I've treated has without question been agoraphobia. Unlike the majority of the other anxiety disorders, agoraphobia is evident at the moment of first contact. The veneer of agoraphobes is thin and their panic-driven behaviors are easy to discern.

Typically, the agoraphobes who choose to consult with me believe that work-related stressors are instigators of their condition. Perhaps, they surmise, if the workplace environment can be changed to accommodate their needs, then their stress-related problems will collapse or vanish. Since I'm a career and workplace psychologist, I appear to these clients to be an appropriate choice for intervention.

Other Phobias

Other phobias, including "specific" phobias, are also easy to spot. For instance, if a person seeks treatment for an elevator phobia (not an uncommon diagnosis, I've found, in the high-rise financial district of San Francisco) the problem is clearly articulated in the initial telephone contact. People who suffer from a flying phobia have often known for years that it's an unyielding issue, making air travel unimaginable. Usually a very pressing life circumstance, like a new job with travel or a destination wedding, demands that they address and eradicate the phobia expeditiously.

These are specific problems that respond relatively well to specific treatments. There's no reason for a person to continue denying the issue when the phobia has become more than a vexing inconvenience.

What Triggers a Phobia?

Every one of my phobic clients wants to know what caused their phobia. This is a simple question with no easy answer, although my clients sometimes have fascinating ideas of their own about the causes. Certainly traumatic events like being trapped in an elevator or attacked by a dog can be predisposing factors to elevator, closet, or canine phobias. Unexpected panic attacks in a particular environment, even a familiar one, can also make any anxiety-free return to that setting impossible. Agoraphobes often believe that their disorder was brought on this way. Unfortunately, parents can unconsciously serve to create phobias in children with their repeated warnings about the terrible things that happen to those who disobey house rules.

But sometimes unrelated life issues can elicit phobic behavior. For example, my client Simon developed a severe case of social phobia after losing confidence in his abilities when he wasn't promoted as quickly as he'd expected. The disorder kept him from giving public presentations to his management group, and he could only meet with his subordinates one on one. He was on the verge of being terminated when he met with me.

The aptly named "new consumerism" can make many people unravel when they feel they don't measure up. When Donna rode the bus to her marketing job each day, she overheard the conversations of young executives obsessed with increasing their wealth. The stomach-wrenching anxiety she experienced as she compared her successes to theirs forced her to stop riding the bus. Thereafter she refused to ride any public transportation, including airplanes. Her anxiety severely reduced the scope of her world.

Even generalized anxiety disorder (GAD) can be triggered by life problems in surprising ways. Jim developed GAD when he was promoted to a new position, one he had wanted for years. But his ever-increasing new responsibilities had repercussions. Jim couldn't stop worrying about not only his own performance, but also the performance of his corporate division. He lost sleep, couldn't eat, and became increasingly irritable with his confidants. He told me that his body never felt relaxed. This was supposed to be a time for Jim to swagger among his coworkers as chief honcho. Yet here he was sloshing through the worst emotional turbulence of his life.

Diagnostic Dilemmas

A client with one anxiety disorder may also satisfy the diagnostic criteria for another mental disorder, including another anxiety disorder. This is called *comorbidity*. Sometimes specific anxiety disorders are difficult to diagnose because their physical symptoms are not necessarily specific to a particular anxiety. For example, you can have a dry mouth and sweaty palms, which are specific symptoms of anxiety, before going on a date or giving a speech, or while being confronted by a neighbor.

In addition, life circumstances that have led to the development of an anxiety disorder can also lead to other disorders, such as depression or dysthymia. Living in an abusive or alcoholic household can contribute to cognitive processes and belief systems that can result in depressed, anxious thought patterns.

Seeking Help for Agoraphobia and the Referral Process

Significantly, the agoraphobia sufferer is rarely the first to seek help for the disorder. In only 5 percent of the agoraphobia cases I've treated has the first telephone contact been initiated by the client.

Medical personnel, employers, and employee assistance program (EAP) counselors certainly make their share of referrals. But for the most part, mothers, fathers, siblings, cousins, lovers, or concerned friends serve as the first wave of contact.

Each of the phone calls to my office from these "confined companions" has been filled with marked exasperation and disappointment. The voices at the other end of the line are replete with pain, insecurity, concern, and bewilderment, with often only a flicker of positive emotion.

Questions abound: How long will treatment take? How expensive will it be? Now, it's hardly rare for clients to inquire about time and cost in the treatment process. But the life of the family member, companion, or concerned advisor of an agoraphobe, as well as that of the person they're referring, has been markedly interrupted. Quite clearly, they want this fixed fast—at times, it seems, even more than the agoraphobe does.

While the caregivers usually say that they don't want the sufferer to throw away his or her life, a subtext I almost always hear is that they're just bewildered and don't know what to do. These disclosures of assumed powerlessness are among the most disheartening I have listened to. Some caregivers also fear for their own health and sanity if changes aren't made.

Why the Client Doesn't Call

I hasten to point out that a majority of my agoraphobic clients have had an absolute dread of their disorder and have wanted immediate change. They weren't malingerers. But what had kept them from treatment was that they were often too frightened to leave their home environment to seek help. They were sometimes, ironically, terrified of the possibility of change itself.

A plastic surgeon friend told me that he experiences this type of fear with his own patients. They want changes, but are also frightened of the outcome. Computer images of what a surgical outcome will look like certainly help calm them. Even so, sometimes it takes his patients months to adjust to a new "look." Fear of change is common to us all, not just agoraphobes.

Initial Interventions

Well-intentioned family members and friends often believe that they can personally change an agoraphobic. Even the most skeptical companions have truly thought that love, encouragement, and support could thwart the problem. Others have thought that some aggressive, startling jolt to the body, like a slap to the face, might bring the loved one out of the agoraphobic vortex as quickly as he or she got in.

This aggressive approach, by the way, has a history. Lobotomies, insulin therapy, and electro convulsive therapy (ECT, or shock therapy) have all been used to treat mental disorders. So has physical abuse. Indeed, the Hollywood films *Paths of Glory* and *Patton* illustrate this approach. Each film has at least one scene in which high-ranking military officers try to address post-traumatic stress disorder (at the time called "battle fatigue") by slapping the afflicted soldier in the face.

Nevertheless, few if any sufferers can fully address their agoraphobia with either loving encouragement or sobering jolts from significant others. Moreover, physically mistreating agoraphobics under the guise of treatment is not only ridiculous but clearly abusive. The afflicted people need professional help.

Disappointments for the Caregivers

My first contact with the agoraphobic's caregiver is often perplexing and, I suspect, disappointing to them. In trying to be honest with the people I counsel and their family members, I have to inform them that the treatment of agoraphobia is not always as successful as they hope it will be. Even with the armamentarium of knowledge, pharmaceuticals, community resources, and psychotherapeutic techniques currently available, it's hard to predict at the outset who is going to fully recover, or at least improve, and who isn't.

In it's unpredictability, agoraphobia is similar to the substance-related disorders. Just like substance abusers, agoraphobics can fall prey to their problem unexpectedly. An agoraphobe never really knows when the fears, panic, or overwhelming desire to hightail it back home will occur. He or she must learn to live with this and, like the person with a substance abuse disorder, will always be in some kind of recovery. So, too, will the agoraphobe's family members and significant other. If you get nothing else from this book, I hope that you and your companion come to see the importance of putting time and effort every day into a recovery program.

Agoraphobia Is Complex

Agoraphobia is among the most prevalent of the anxiety disorders; according to the Mental Health Report of the Surgeon General, only the classification "specific phobia" is more common. Yet new research suggests that agoraphobia is a more complex anxiety disorder than the others because it doesn't exist alone. Instead, it's defined and framed by another problem, panic disorder.

In the DSM-IV-TR, which is the manual all psychologists use to diagnose mental disorder, agoraphobia is not, by itself, a codable disorder—that is, one with a specific number, or code, in the DSM-IV-TR. Rather, three different disorders utilize the term "agoraphobia": panic disorder without agoraphobia, panic disorder with agoraphobia, and agoraphobia without history of panic disorder. This complexity of classification makes diagnosis and treatment of agora- phobia both intriguing and demanding. These different classifications will be covered in depth in chapter 3.

In addition, there can sometimes be distinctive fluctuations in the symptoms of an agoraphobic. I've worked with some who have been confined to their homes for months and then have a period of time when they appeared to be symptom-free. Others have a period of years in their lives when they are agoraphobic. Then that period seems to pass and they are able to function reasonably well forever.

To a caregiving companion, the gyrations in the agoraphobic's condition can look deliberately meanspirited. When your companion appears to be getting over the problem, then regresses without warning, the most optimistic of caregivers can fall into despair. A caregiver named Daisy told me that all of her effort felt like just a "spit in the ocean" when her companion relapsed.

Agoraphobics and Dependency

Agoraphobics tend to have some history of or tendency toward dependency. Most have expressed a desire for someone else to handle the more difficult tasks in their lives. Furthermore, they're usually starving for approval and the reassurance that they will not be abandoned. So when they latch onto a caregiver, it's torturous for them to let go. Caregivers use phrases like "joined at the hip" or "my coattails are tugged at" to describe their experience with their companions. You might be feeling that your relationship with your companion has become an emotional minefield.

The dependency needs of some agoraphobics can also lead to their developing inappropriate or dysfunctional relationships, including marriages, that are based more on fear than love. It can take patience and effort on behalf of both agoraphobe and companion to restore a spirit of affection to the relationship.

Why I Wrote This Book

In my view, since both substance abuse and agoraphobia involve the family and significant others, perhaps both need to be treated as family problems as well as individual ones. But while there are many books and self-help organizations (like Al-Anon) for companions of people with substance abuse, there isn't much available for the care-givers of agoraphobics. In most cases, the self-sacrificing companion has a bruising litany of frustrating experiences and nothing to compare them to. It was because of this lack that I decided to write this book.

The only books addressing agoraphobia that I found that were similar in scope to this one were texts published by Kenneth Strong (1997) and Karen Williams (1993). Both Strong and Williams are recovering agoraphobes with much insight into the disorder. Williams suggests that caregivers develop attitudes of "acceptance, understanding, sincerity, compassion, encouragement, patience, recognition of the companion's accomplishments, trustworthiness, and participation in the treatment." That's nicely outlined, but as you probably know, it's nearly impossible to achieve.

Unfortunately, both books overlook some of the more complex issues of agoraphobic family dynamics, particularly dependency and codependency—subjects I'll address in this book. Furthermore, this book is written from the perspective of a psychologist in a chair in a treatment room (or a living room or bedroom as the case may be). So it's based on my listening to the different stories rather than participating in them.

For some general ideas on how to live with a companion who has a mental health problem, consider reading Lynn Bradley's book (2000) on how to live with and love a manic-depressive. She aptly describes how her husband's mental disorder affected not only their life together, but also the lives of their children. While the book is not without its flaws, it does speak to some of the tragic as well as comic experiences that companions share with their caregivers.

Who Should Read This Book?

This book is not written for agoraphobics. Instead, its mission is to support and educate their family members, primary caregivers, companions, and support people—helpers, if you will. That's not to say that people with agoraphobia won't be interested in this material. In fact, they might be very curious to understand more about how the family or relationship dynamic is intertwined with their disorder. But in general, other books will prove to be most useful for agoraphobics. Both Bourne's *The Anxiety and Phobia Workbook* (2000) and Zuercher-White's *An End to Panic: Breakthrough Techniques for Overcoming Panic Disorder* (1998) are certainly relevant and useful.

Specifically this book hopes to:

1. Help you to clarify your feelings about the predicament you're in

2. Give you a new understanding of your behavior in the context of a family system that is currently unbalanced

3. Help you determine whether or not your behavior is enabling the condition of the agoraphobic

4. Provide you with valuable, up-to-date information about agoraphobia and other associated anxiety disorders, and the different treatments that are available

5. Give you practical information about different types of support services that you may choose to use as well

6. Provide you with behavioral and cognitive behavioral techniques that you can actually practice with your companion and that will serve to empower both of you.

The basic premise of this book is that you ought to do what's necessary to provide support to your agoraphobic companion while keeping yourself healthy. Any substance-abuse counselor will tell you that it is the caregivers who often become the most physically enfeebled and mentally ill in a family where there is a substance abuser. So it may be when the family contains an agoraphobe. This book will give you knowledge and techniques to help you address your own feelings and issues of codependency, self-esteem, and guilt and forgive yourself for what you're simply not able to work out with your agoraphobic companion.

You're Not Alone

The book will also let you know that you're not alone. Since many agoraphobics are confined to limited territories, their lives can be very lonely. Most agoraphobics who have some support from others become extraordinarily dependent on that support. This can lead to other problems, which will be discussed in detail later.

Caregivers can feel wretchedly lonely, too. You may not have met many people with whom to share your experience: agoraphobic family caregivers don't have the community of support resources available to alcoholic family caregivers. You may feel a heightened sense of uniqueness because you've not had the experience of other caregivers confiding in you.

Agoraphobia Is Difficult to Understand

What's particularly characteristic of this disorder is that you and other helpers probably have little understanding of what your agoraphobic loved one is experiencing. You've been hunkering in the bunker with someone who perceives the world outside the home as a terribly frightening place. You probably don't resonate with this, or at least the world doesn't feel as threatening to you as it does to the person you're living with or assisting. Likewise, your agoraphobic companion probably has little understanding of what the presence of this disorder is doing to you.

Unlike many other psychological disorders, agoraphobia can confine you to the household along with your agoraphobic companion. Your inability to escape, travel, comfortably relax, or operate a normal, functioning lifestyle or household can be enormously depressing, making your life feel out of control. Moreover, you may not be caring for yourself in a wholesome manner. You may be acting out—possibly engaging in your own pattern of substance abuse—in an attempt to cope with the difficulties in your life.

In addition, you probably feel incompetent a lot of the time. You know how much effort you're putting into caregiving and you expect better results. Keep in mind, however, that you're only half of this relationship. You'll profit by accepting responsibility only for your side of the experience.

Many of you know that it seems unacceptable for you to complain about your predicament. Though you may need some way to express your feelings of frustration and self-pity, your support network may be burned out on your constant talk about your circumstances. In any of these events, this book will help you to become mindful of and address activity that's counterproductive to your helping capacity and to your own well-being.

Self-Examination Can Help

So this book is going to ask you to look at yourself and your behavior patterns as it gives you information and direction about relating to your agoraphobe. This book proposes to validate your efforts while helping you understand how you lost control of some or all of your life and how you can get it back.

This book is a response to the cries for help that I've heard from caregivers over the years. Whether it was emotional support, caring from others, time and life management techniques, or just the ability to keep the family intact, the companions have had a plethora of unmet needs.

Complex problems like agoraphobia should be treated by a professional person who knows about the disorder and the available treatments. But a book like this may make it possible for all readers to better understand the phenomena surrounding agoraphobia. It should also allow you to apply some new strategies for governing your own life.

Above all, I hope that this book will give you the empowering feeling that you *can* cope with the circumstances and the life changes that have been brought into your life. Reading this book is another step toward your own recovery.

1

How Agoraphobia Affects You and Your Family

This chapter discusses the myriad ways agoraphobia can inveigle its way into your life and stymie your sense of order. I'll share some examples of how families and designated caregivers have coped with this strange, kooky new phenomenon in their lives. This material will also illustrate why your caregiving roles and responsibilities drain you emotionally. Some of the examples may feel quite familiar; others perhaps not so much. All will disclose something of the tension that others in similar circumstances experience.

We begin by addressing the disruptions to your own life brought on by a companion's agoraphobia. In addition to the inconveniences that may be a part of the experience, perhaps the most difficult aspect of becoming a caregiver is the interruption of your own sense of who you are in the world.

The Interruption of Your Life Roles

Throughout life, we all undertake a variety of distinctive roles, almost like actors in a theater. These roles we assume serve to establish our identity: a notion of who we are and who we hope to become. We sometimes refer to our identity as our sense of self.

Significantly, throughout life, we all play ever-changing and sometimes contradictory parts. But in the establishment of our identity, we seek out a continuity and sameness between the various roles that we played early in life with those that we come to play later. This predictability, according to Erik Erikson (1950), helps to lead us to the unconfused establishment of our identity, which is among our most important life tasks.

Our identity helps to keep us well focused and gives us a foundation from which to make demanding life decisions. Knowing who we are keeps us resilient. And the lack of a clearly defined identity leads to what Erikson has referred to as *role confusion* or identity diffusion.

Role Confusion

Self-doubt originates in role confusion. A lack of clarity about who we are tends to make us second-guess many important decisions in our lives. We frequently notice this in the beginning of professional training. Fledgling lawyers, physicians, software engineers, chefs, and payroll clerks may all second-guess themselves before they develop the feelings of expertise particular to their professional identity. Identity thus allows us to develop authenticity and competence in what we say and do in our professional lives.

Did You Expect to Be a Caregiver?

I dwell on role confusion for a moment because it helps explain why the role you've assumed as caregiver may be so psychologically demanding. You probably have a belief that your life experiences will help you handle the ups and downs of your daily living. If you've taken even a beginning psychology course, you've probably also been taught to believe that your life will proceed in certain well-defined stages.

However, when you assumed the role of caregiver, an unanticipated road hazard got thrown across your life path. Suddenly your life stages don't appear to be so clear-cut. You can't be entirely sure when you'll resume traveling your life path according to the map you've created for yourself. Your experience is not unlike discovering that you have a child with a severe disability or a parent with Alzheimer's, or that you have a catastrophic illness. Your misfortunes clash with your plans.

The role change forces you to accept that which is so unacceptable and unexpected to you. It may put you into some degree of denial. And it's probably quite difficult for you not to feel burdened by your loved one's agoraphobia. The burden you feel can and will make you view your companion, from time to time at least, with feelings of anger, contempt, tentativeness, or indifference.

Challenges to Your Identity

The role that you play with someone close to you can also force you to confront some of the long-held ideas you have about yourself. If you feel that you're an athletic, strong, decisive human being, you may expect that you'll become a sort of champion to the person you're caring for. It can be disheartening and perplexing to find that you're not as effective a caregiver or amateur therapist as you thought you were. Maybe you think of yourself as patient and compassionate, a self-image that can be challenged by any hostile reactions you have toward your companion.

Making matters worse, criticism of your efforts can come from different corners. Any number of people (including your companion and other family members) may reproach you for the degree of support you're offering even while you believe you're doing everything imaginable. You'll want to enlist the assistance of others around you. But even those who disparage your efforts won't necessarily offer much time and support to either you or your companion.

Caregiving Is Disruptive

Many people have the notion that they can plan for disruptions in life. Whether they're painful ones, like surgical procedures, or joyous ones, like family-making, such planning gives us a sense of control, however misguided.

We also attempt to control our lives by agreeing or refusing to assist others who need us. For example, your friends could tell you that it might not be a good time for them to take care of your dog. My colleagues might remove themselves from certain committee responsibilities by informing me that they're having a very demanding week. You may not be willing to carpool with someone whose schedule differs enough from yours to make the experience inconvenient.

Since caregiving is almost never planned for, it often elicits strong feelings of being out of control. The disruption you've experienced in caring for your agoraphobic companion was not part of your plan and probably feels like it came upon you out of nowhere. It can impact your ability to care for the other important people in your life. It can make you feel like you're deprived of some of the life experiences you had planned for.

Don't Expect Validation from Others

If you're in the middle of the caregiving process, you probably know that caregivers aren't given much validation from society for their efforts. Other cultures may value caregiving, but American culture usually doesn't. This most demanding and important of life roles will go unnoticed by most. Even family members will forget from time to time to acknowledge the effort that you make as a primary caregiver.

So if your life mission involves achieving some sort of social recognition, becoming a caregiver may lead to serious anger, frustration, and depression. If you expect that other significant people in your life will validate your role, you'll inevitably feel some degree of alienation from them when you feel you're not appropriately acknowledged by them.

Not only are your sense of self and your life path disrupted, but your experience also feels unfamiliar and precipitate. In the late 1980s, the term "sandwich generation" was used to characterize a population of people who were not only raising their own children but also caring for aging parents. The vast interest in this concept was the result of people's needing to know how to balance care of their elders with care of their children. At the same time, these people needed to feel that they weren't alone in their efforts.

While the disruption to your life's predictability is probably among the most difficult parts of caregiving, there are other complications. In becoming a good caregiver, you'll find that the balance of your life may be lost. Your role with regard to the person you are caring for will change. You will have less time for yourself and you may not take care of your own needs as well as you had earlier. And your sense of personal empowerment can vanish.

See Caregiving as a New Path

Yet you may find that in the caregiving process, you'll also learn something new and significant about yourself. You may find that sacrificing, providing earnest support, and practicing compassion for somebody else has its own personal and spiritual rewards. You may learn that you don't necessarily need to expect something in return for your caregiving. You might learn a great deal of new information about your community. You may find yourself presented with new educational experiences and in the company of people whom you would have never expected to meet in the past.

Effective Caregiving and Character Type

While you adjust to becoming a caregiver, it may help to reflect upon the type of person you are. To be sure, people with particular personality types do have an easier time with caregiving. People who are competitive, withholding, angry, narcissistic, prone to abandonment, and unable to comfort tend not to be natural caregivers. Likewise, some people with personality disorders are rarely able to provide comfort and structure for others.

Problematic Caregiving Personalities

In *The Anxiety and Phobia Workbook* (2000), Bourne puts names to six different types of personalities that may have difficulty becoming effective caregivers. These names came from earlier work by Arthur Hardy (1976), who was the founder of TERRAP (short for Territorial Apprehensiveness), a recognized, effective means for treating agoraphobia. These personality types are:

1. The overly capable type

2. The overly dictatorial, domineering type

3. The overly protective type

4. The overly critical type

5. The overly quiet, inhibited type

6. The overly objective type

The first three of these types, according to Bourne, are variations on the theme of codependency, which will be discussed in a later chapter. The other types don't necessarily elicit a degree of codependency, but are still problematic to the agoaphobic's recovery process.

In my work with agoraphobics and caregivers I have found three other less-than-effective types that I'll add to the list. These are:

7. The "it's all about me" type

8. The overly worried type

9. The discounting type

The Overly Capable Type

Overly capable caregivers move in and take charge. They're responsible. In Bourne's word, they work to "fix" the problems. They also need recognition that they're something akin to geniuses. Caregiver Doug loved to impress others, especially his companion's therapist (me), with his knowledge of the disorder. While he was committed to helping, he also inhibited his agoraphobic companion from developing any sense of confidence or independence.

If you're an overly capable type, like Doug, you need to step back and learn how to become more of a partner in the process, restraining yourself from doing too much. Your highly capable posturing could distress your companion, exacerbating his or her already low self-esteem.

You want to help inculcate in your companion a feeling of some degree of control, which will enable them to approach their problem pragmatically. If you can help them with that, then you can also better help them practice the recovery activities in this book.

When I work with overly capable caregivers, I try to establish them in some kind of a partnership with me. This usually works. Doug had some tendency to try to discredit me; he really gloried in his own expertise. Still, by and large, he put a great measure of energy into the caregiving process, and our partnership worked.

The Overly Dictatorial, Domineering Type

Domineering caregivers want control and power. They perceive agoraphobia not as an emotional mystery but as a lack of motivational will and discipline. The degree to which these caregivers are able to elicit fear and inhibition in their agoraphobic companions has led me to call them "Sherman tanks." There's an underlying rigidity to this type of caregiver, who may feel hostility toward the agoraphobic companion or toward the family in general.

Sharon thrived on confrontation and relished enforcing her caste-iron point of view. Her agoraphobic sister was left unable to respond to her with any degree of spontaneity. She was never able to learn to get beyond her fears because she felt she was supposed to do everything Sharon's way.

Dictators are usually caring, but they need to learn to unwind and be better listeners. Sharon grudgingly accepted my referral for her own personal therapy to help her understand the roots of her own anger and need to control her sister. This effort eventually allowed for a better relationship between the two of them. However, Sharon's complaints and negative feelings about agoraphobia continued to make her a less-than-effective caregiver.

The Overly Protective Type

The overly protective caregiver tries to satisfy all the basic needs of his or her companion. In this sense, these caregivers resemble the overly capable type. However, one of the distinctive aspects of this type is an overwhelming need to be liked by others, especially the agoraphobic companion. So while these caregivers are responding to both the basic and the higher-order needs of their companions, they're also making sure that their own needs for love are met. Accordingly, they'll allow their companions to become more and more dependent. That strategy ensures that they snare a degree of love and satisfaction from the caregiving experience.

Joyce received inordinate validation of her own identity by remaining in a protective role for her daughter. Though she was dreadfully inefficient in looking after herself, caring for her daughter guaranteed that she would have love in her life forever.

To be sure, many helpers can become overly protective. From time to time I've had to caution my own first-year graduate students against assuming this type of role. The best recourse for overly protective people is to understand that their needs are not, in the end, necessarily going to be met by their companion.

The Overly Critical Type

Overly critical caregivers have often been subjected to a lifetime of negative judgments by significant people in their lives, typically their parents. Unfortunately, they believe that criticism is a blessing to their companion in much the same way that some parents believe that constant chastising is the very best way to raise a child.

But agoraphobics are filled with fears, and tend to be nervous about how people feel toward them already. Agoraphobics can't stand to have someone lurking over their shoulder, passing judgment. In fact, it's often the judgment of others, particularly in times of transition, that elicits the first panic attacks. So overly critical "eye-rollers" are really ineffective at providing the kind of supportive care the agoraphobic needs.

If you find that you're uncontrollably critical of your companion's many fears, you might not be in the best position to provide useful care. You should either seek your own form of professional consultation or shepherd others into the fold to assist you—or both.

The Overly Quiet, Inhibited Type

The overly quiet type tends to be somewhat introverted and shy, wishing mostly to avoid conflict. Since any measure of confrontation is aversive to them and they typically need assistance in expressing their own feelings, they have difficulty helping their companions express feelings. If you find that you can't express your own feelings to your companion in a polite and dignified way, then you may not be allowing your companion to do so either.

Think of it this way: you're not providing the kind of stimulation that your companion needs, and at the same time you're stifling yourself. The degree to which you're unable to express yourself will contribute to feelings of anger toward your companion, but your tendency will be to walk away from the situation rather than trying to settle it in a mutually respectful way with your companion. Joining an assertiveness training seminar or communication support group certainly could help.

The Overly Objective Type

The overly objective caregiver believes that everything can be reduced to simple, logical data points. Randall thought there "must be" reasons for his wife to be agoraphobic. As a supremely logical person, he believed that I should cut through the psychological thicket to get to the root of the cause of his wife's disorder—and thereby cure it. My explanations of the origins of agoraphobia through different personal vulnerabilities seemed too vague and unscientific to him.

Unfortunately, there's no way that your agoraphobic companion is going to be able to explain in the midst of a panic attack exactly why it is happening, other than to say that this circumstance elicits a panic attack. You can't "logic" him or her out of having the attack, and the challenge for the overly objective–type caregiver is to learn not to try.

The "It's All about Me" Type

These caregivers tend to see the companion's problem in light of how it affects them rather than how it affects their companion. The agoraphobia is all about them, not about the person with the problem, and they can't seem to get beyond this. Such a caregiver feels that the companion has unfairly interrupted the caregiver's life and career.

This class of caregiver usually puts clearly articulated time limits and/or spending limits on the care they plan to give. This caregiver also has a tendency to put the entire relationship "on the line" if the companion doesn't stay with a treatment program or demonstrate at least some improvement. Any relapse almost always terminates the caregiving and, possibly, the relationship.

I've counseled parents with agoraphobic children who were too busy to seek out assistance and who allowed their children to just stay at home alone. I've met with others who are reluctant to make any commitment about caregiving. Interestingly, even though these caregivers had no time to contribute to their companions, they would still argue with the companions about their care.

The agoraphobe companion usually recognizes the caretaker's lack of commitment either by intuition or experience. Don't forget, agoraphobes always fear abandonment. And with the "it's all about me" type of caregiver, they feel that if they don't make some sort of positive change, their caregiving companion is going to throw in the towel.

It's a situation fraught with conflict and danger. On one hand, agoraphobics need a companion. On the other, they're made to feel that they're a burden, and that quite possibly they're going to lose a familiar love object, family member, or companion. This pressure seems to create a turbulent, vicious downward spiral as the agoraphobe becomes ever more fearful of their companion's leaving. Jeremy told me recently that the song that reverberated for him was Kenny Rogers' "Ruby" about a wife "taking her love to town" because her disabled husband couldn't satisfy her. Clearly this was not a propitious situation. Caregivers need to regularly demonstrate, through words and actions, that they won't give up on or abandon their companions.

The Overly Worried Type

Since there's probably some genetic component to agoraphobia, it's not surprising that in an agoraphobic family there will be more than one categorical worrier. Overly worried caregivers are averse to change. They worry that their labor's not going to amount to much good, so they're better off doing nothing.

The worried types have a tendency to disregard new therapies and medications and alternative techniques like bodywork, yoga, stretching, and meditation. Thus, they can be reluctant to help their companions practice some of the techniques that are recommended by therapists and other consultants. They tend to imagine negative consequences.

In addition to worrying about the ultimate effectiveness of the different interventions available for agoraphobics, they also worry about the time and money that the treatment is demanding. As a therapist, I've found them to be difficult to work with.

Fortunately, this kind of person can be helped with an avalanche of educational material. They can also be helped by examining, with the aid of another, their own patterns of worry. Most of these caregivers feel that their worry undermines their own health and well-being as well as that of their companion. They can be well served by stopping the type of negative, self-defeating chatter that they give themselves. Simple changes in language can help take caregivers out of the realm of incessant, torturous worry. Rather than saying, "This whole situation is a complete disaster," a caregiver can learn to say, "This situation is going to need attention." The change in language cuts the problem down to its proper size.

E. M. Hallowell (1997) found that worry could be addressed with a practice called *rational intervention*. He created three steps that he calls the *EPR technique*, for "evaluate," "plan," and "remediate." Essentially, worriers need to make a reasonably fair and unbiased evaluation of the situation they're in. Then they need to develop a plan to address their dilemma. Finally, they need to implement the plan, remediating the problem with their plan or some variation of it.

EPR is useful because it can help to take worry away. It forces the caregiver out of his or her own head and into the creation of an action strategy. Further, EPR allows for the variation and flexibility in caregiving.

The Discounting Type

A discounter is, frankly, in denial about the companion's condition. This type tends to literally dismiss either the seriousness of the problem or the specific fears, issues, and behaviors of the agoraphobe. It's not just that they tend to disbelieve the companion: they can also disbelieve that any such problem as agoraphobia can exist. They can be dictatorial as well.

The denial of mental health problems by even the most well-educated and sophisticated people is epidemic. Parents don't want to believe that they have a child who might have attention deficit disorder, or be learning disabled. Parents, teachers, and deans of students around the country remain in outrageous denial about the abuse of drugs and alcohol among young people, writing off adolescents' problems as simply growing pains.

Discounters, like overly domineering types, believe that people just need to try harder. When a child is learning disabled, their remedy is to demand more hard work. When drugs and alcohol are a problem among their adolescent children, they take away the keys to the car. They don't seek treatment for themselves or their children. Most significantly, they don't readily admit that there's a problem in the family. Discounters frankly need strong doses of education to confront their denial. The resources at the conclusion of this book will help.

What Type of Caregiver Are You?

Now that you've read through this list, are there any caregiver types you identify with? Search your memory for any images of conflict or dysfunction between you and your companion. As you reflect upon the different descriptions of caregivers for agoraphobics, write down a description of the kind of caregiver you feel you are. This outline might help:

1. Find words and phrases that describe who you are; use terms from the preceding pages if they seem to apply. Then, describe yourself as a caregiver in a paragraph or two.

2. Write down a few of the most memorable exchanges you've had with your companion, both good and bad.

3. Write down descriptions of the behavior patterns that you exhibit with your companion. These could be encouraging, avoiding, or criticizing patterns, among others.

4. Write down your concerns about the caregiving process. What are your most troubling obsessions and worries?

5. Now, list the thoughts and the feelings you have about your companion, both positive and negative.

6. Write down any additional thoughts and feelings you have about your current circumstances.

Can you hear your own voice in this exercise? Upon further review, do you appear to fit into any of the nine caregiver types just described? Do you find yourself in more than one of the categories? As the final piece of this exercise, write down a list of any thoughts, feelings, behaviors, language, and interaction patterns you would like to change to be a better person and caregiver. Use this list as a personal contract for yourself—a reminder of your commitment to harvest something unique and positive from caregiving.

The Benefits of Caregiving

By assessing yourself, you'll learn about yourself in your role as a caregiver. There will be other benefits as well. As you provide support as a caregiver, you'll learn a bit of psychology; you'll also learn how to help another person practice new skills. If you encourage your agoraphobic companion to attempt new relaxation activities like meditation, yoga, or the "quieting reflex," which will be covered in other chapters, you may find that you learn these skills as well and apply them to your own life.

You'll also be able to understand new breakthroughs in medication and other treatments for anxiety. And you'll be able to better communicate with health-care professionals. Hopefully, you'll also learn to care a bit for your own health, to say "no" without feeling guilty, and to create appropriate boundaries and be demanding when that becomes important for you.

There will be dilemmas in your caregiving career. You'll be frustrated for all the reasons I've mentioned. But you don't have to see your life as a scrap heap. You can feel well rewarded for the offering you make to a person you love. You will find that you'll be able to create some very real means to assisting your companion. You'll also find that there are some guidelines you can develop for yourself that will help you to gather some degree of control over your own life.

Some Longer Cases

With the benefits and challenges of caregiving in mind, I want to discuss several clients I have worked with whose caregivers made extraordinary adjustments to their lives. These cases all address agoraphobia and caregiving in the context of family dynamics. They all speak to the disruptions individuals face when they become caregivers. As you read the cases, try to consider whether or not you fit into any of the roles. You will meet these people again throughout the text, so I've given you some details to remember them by.

The first case speaks to the interaction between family members when they're in denial about having an agoraphobic child. A number of the different types of caregiving roles are apparent here. The family's crucial issue is a long-standing one, related to family members' fears that something catastrophic will happen to them. A history of worry among the family members, and the family dynamics that ensue, demonstrate how the agoraphobia becomes a family problem.

The second case deals with a child who is put into the role of caregiving and comes to resent it, upon reflection, later in life. I've worked with a number of adults who continued to struggle with the early loss of their childhood innocence. To some extent, they feel as if their childhood was taken away from them and that they had to grow up far too quickly.

The final case concerns a young couple wherein one of the partners, out of love and devotion, tries to make everything work out.

This case illustrates issues that are often part of the caregiving process in a loving life partnership. It also speaks to the complicated aberrations that take place when the caregiver doesn't get the results he or she expects.

Stressors and Agoraphobia

There appear to be no specific stressors that are predictably related to the onset of agoraphobia. I've searched endlessly for such stressors, using hypnosis and other techniques, to no avail. But clearly some degree of stress and anxiety takes place prior to the outbreak of the panic attacks that serve as the background for the agoraphobia. Disruption in relationships or the loss of safety at home or work may serve as possible antecedents to the emergence of agoraphobia, but again, the effect of such changes is not predictable.

Transitions and Agoraphobia

In treating agoraphobes, one commonality I've found is that they often feel acute strains and conflicts about life transitions. Leaving home or not, getting married or not, terminating one job or relationship for another, all serve to illustrate this point. Interestingly, the age of onset of agoraphobia has been seen to occur most commonly either between the ages of fifteen to twenty or between thirty to forty (Marks 1970).

It's not surprising to me that the greatest incidence of agoraphobia occurrs at these two periods in a person's life. The earlier age bracket is a time of transition between leaving home and going off to college or military service or settling into a new working pattern. The transitional choices that people make later in life also have a profound emotional impact. Between the ages of thirty and forty individuals may be having children or deciding whether or not to stay with a particular career. This time span leaves people ripe for unanticipated anxiety or agoraphobia.

Freud pointed out that our most demanding life decisions are related to our love and our work (*lieben und arbeiten*); so we find that agoraphobia seems to emerge around transitions related to relationships and personal and work identity.

Dan's Case — A Young Man in Transition

Dan is a good example of a young man who fits into this pattern of agoraphobia that emerges around stress-related issues: making a transition into a work identity while struggling to decide whether to leave the family home. His situation also shows how the family's involvement and the caregiving process begin early in the agoraphobic experience, even before any kind of treatment begins.

The Referral from Janet

I was introduced to Dan and his condition by a typical telephone inquiry from his older sister Janet. (As I suggested earlier, referring calls from family members of agoraphobes are common.) Within the above classifications of caregivers, Janet might be seen as a combination of the "overly worried" and the "it's all about me" types.

Two things were a little unusual for me about my conversation with Janet. First, she was very upset on the phone; she had an enormously difficult time telling me what the problem was and whom she was phoning for. She was at once angry, tearful, and frustrated about how her life was out of control. Most people who refer others to me don't sound as upset as she was. But as I noted, she had the "it's all about me" personality type. Second, she focused on her family.

Janet said her entire family seemed to be falling apart. The problem with her brother was affecting everyone. What Janet recounted was that Dan's life and the life of the family changed instantly, in one day, nine months or so into his managerial job tenure. On that day, in which, she said, "nothing, absolutely nothing out of the ordinary was occurring," Dan froze with fear in his car immediately after he entered the employee parking lot at his company.

Janet described her brother as a twenty-three-year-old college graduate who had been a successful plant manager trainee for a silicon chip manufacturer in San Jose, California. He had been doing just fine, but the family had an undercurrent of worry about how he would measure up in the work world.

She added that throughout most of his life, Dan had been "a little jumpy and hypervigilant," and even paranoid, always waiting for something bad to happen. Everyone was concerned that Dan would not measure up to the family's expectations of him.

Janet noted that Dan's nervous tension seemed to run in the family. She readily admitted that even she had shown signs of nervousness over the years: she habitually bit her fingernails while she watched television and picked at her toenails when she read in her bed in the evening. She, like others in the family, was dreadfully insecure about the future and almost always worried about money. She had no sense of what amount of money would make her feel comfortable.

Janet characterized her father as a "tortured, neurotic mess." Her once well-meaning, reasonably well-contained mother, she said, had recently transformed into an angry, whiskey-breathed harridan. "Mother has lost it," she lamented. I momentarily considered that the mother could be a dictatorial type who couldn't get her way.

Janet's experience of her parents was that they always felt that they needed to protect themselves in some fashion. They feared that their children would eventually disgrace them. "It was like they never trusted the universe, and now their fears were coming home to roost."

She remarked that the family typically disavowed the existence of any problems and that all family matters were kept well contained. She, her parents, and Dan thought that Dan's nervous ups and downs were really pretty typical for someone his age. She added wryly that everyone in the family had felt that way for the past six or seven years.

Janet realized now that the family had probably been in denial for years about "a whole bunch of stuff," including Dan's behavior. The parents had placed Janet in the position of getting some help, or at least relief, for Dan and the family. Obviously, they all felt that she was a capable type. I tried to calm her down enough to relate Dan's story to me. She tried.

The Episode

Janet told me that when Dan drove into his parking lot at work, he said he thought his entire body was "seizing up." He imagined that he was having either a heart attack, a nervous breakdown, or an allergic reaction to some breakfast sausages he had eaten. He did have food allergies and he knew his heart sped up when he ingested MSG or anything like it.

Regardless of the cause, he couldn't move. His heart was racing and nothing around him felt like it was real. He felt like he was in a bubble, looking out at the world. His hands were trembling violently; he was unable to open the car door to get himself out. He sat in the car pretending to listen to the radio news reports, ridiculously attempting to smile at onlookers.

As he continued to sit, Janet reported, beads of lukewarm sweat came down his brow. He felt faint, and intuited that if he exited the car and started to walk into the plant, he would pass out. He didn't want to embarrass himself further by exposing his own "personal brand of lifelong nuttiness" to the rest of the company. All of the employees, including his supervisees, were just coming to work; everyone would notice, and he would be so humiliated that he would be unable to meet his colleagues face to face ever again.

Dan was also sure that if he passed out, no one would help him, even if they had the medical wherewithal to do so. Without help, he was concerned he would die—most probably, he surmised, by swallowing his tongue or choking on the sausages he had just eaten.

After what seemed like an eternity, the episode ended somewhat more gradually than it began. It was a panic attack, and all panic attacks finally come to an end, usually in just a few minutes. Though he had calmed down, Dan felt he was never going to be able to get out of the car and enter the plant. Therefore he restarted his car's engine and began to drive back home. He still felt nauseous and light-headed; his legs hurt from shaking.

Janet said that Dan had really wanted to return to the company and tend to work that day. He thought he might relax and pull himself together with a cup of tea or decaffeinated coffee, so he drove to a familiar coffee shop about two miles from the plant. There he was able to get out of the car and go inside, but he was unable to order anything from the waitress. He felt frozen again, speechless, and he had another attack, although this one was not as severe as the first. He described this experience to Janet as akin to viewing the world as if he were in a fishbowl rather than a bubble.

After this attack passed, Dan composed himself, rose slowly from the counter stool, and walked to a pay phone. He called Janet at work and asked her to rescue him: he didn't want to burden his parents. He was terrified to drive home and he knew he couldn't go to work now, even if she drove him there.

Initial Attempts at Caregiving

So that was Janet's introduction to the role of caregiver. The ire in her tone told me she didn't want this role. She just wanted everything fixed. (Indeed, I've never met a caregiver who relished the idea of becoming a self-sacrificing companion.) She recalled that on the day of Dan's first panic attack, she didn't want to leave work to help. She didn't initially feel that it was necessary to come to Dan's rescue. She also resented the fact that she was always the one who was called upon in a family crisis—the "strong one."

Janet told me that her private fear was that no one else was going to have the strength to help and that she would be forced to be in this situation for years. She had been attending to Dan before and after her own work for two weeks, and the family continued to pressure her to help out with caregiving.

Returning to her narrative, Janet remembered that when she got Dan's call, she tried to get him to relax by telling him that everything would be all right. He responded with a lot of "I can'ts." So

Janet, with a combination of concern and anger, left her job and drove to the coffee shop. She found Dan frozen in a booth, with his head in his hands, sweating, and afraid to move without someone next to him. She again tried to convince him that everything was going to be all right, and that he could try to go to work and tell his superiors that he had had a bad case of food poisoning. He rejected this idea with anger, tears, and frustration, and begged her to take him home. She reluctantly helped him walk out of the coffee shop and took him home in her car.

Janet told me that Dan had not returned to work, but had been calling in sick for the past two weeks. The company wanted to know when he was going to return to work. They also wanted a medical excuse for his absence. To help Dan with his medical excuse Janet canvassed her friends and got my name from some of her coworkers who had attended a lecture I had given on stress and anxiety in the workplace. Janet thought that Dan might have some kind of work-related stress or phobia.

I inquired whether Dan might be able to come to my office with someone driving him. But that was out of the question at this point. The family, especially Janet, wanted me to come to the house so they could all meet me.

Contact with Dan

By the time I arrived for my first visit, Dan had been confined to the house for three weeks. He wasn't willing to go out, except after dark, when he drove his car for two to three hours in an area that was approximately one mile square. (I'm struck by the number of my clients who have this particular behavior pattern of driving after dark, alone.)

Walking into Dan's home, I reflected that there was some benefit to breaking out of the traditional psychotherapeutic container and making house calls. I had enough experience with agoraphobics to know that a first visit generally occurred in the home and even, at times, in a "safe" room. Still, at the moment I felt more like a visiting nurse or probation officer than a psychologist.

Dan lived at his parents' home, although Janet had moved out. When I arrived, mother, father, Janet, Dan, and his best friend, Sid, were all there. No one seemed sure how to greet me, though they had high expectations of what I could do. I felt like I was regarded as the Lone Ranger or some kind of superhero who was going to solve what was clearly a family problem. Conversely, I also felt like an intruder.

The family was distraught and desperate; they looked like they had been through a wringer. They talked about Dan as if he were severely physically as well as emotionally disabled, almost like he was immobile and confined to a wheelchair. They tended to his every need.

Before I met with Dan, I spent a few minutes with his parents, mostly so I wouldn't be interrupted when I met with him alone. His mother was frustrated because Dan didn't seem like he wanted to get better, and she felt she had to leave her place of employment several times a day to come home and check up on him. He didn't appear to be willing to return to work. All he did was stay at home and sleep, and that appeared to be all he wanted to do.

Dan's mother said she felt like her home was a prison; her son's problem had become her problem. She took time to reassure me that she was a good mother. Dan's father was fairly passive but also somewhat resistant to treatment. He didn't want to pressure Dan, but he did want the problem solved. He also didn't want this process to cost too much: he talked about my fee three times during the course of my visit. And of course, everyone agreed that the treatment shouldn't take much time. You'll meet Dan and Janet throughout the book as we explore the complex interactions and expectations that caregivers and their agoraphobe companions share.

John's Case—The "Family Hero"

John's case illustrates the circumstances of a very young caregiver trying to keep his somewhat dysfunctional family intact.

John's father was a highly successful cardiologist in Denver, Colorado. He had two children, an attractive home, and a wife who could not leave the house without him. His wife would stay home knitting and watching her "stories" on television all day, and demanded that the children come home immediately after school to keep her company. If they were not home at the appointed hour, she would begin to have moderate panic attacks, which she interpreted as heart attacks. She would then call her husband to come home immediately: she felt she was close to dying and, since he was a cardiologist, he would know how to resuscitate her.

This scenario was a problem. Dad's schedule could not handle these disruptions, and he, as well as his wife, became more and more demanding of the children. As bright and as sophisticated as these parents were, they were unaware of the error of putting this kind of responsibility on the children. They expected the children to play a helping role in caring for their mother, and that was that.

When he was young, John didn't mind the demand to be home too much. But as he grew older, he found himself becoming increasingly angry and resentful that he could not have his own teenage life. His sister was four years younger and had not yet developed any animosity over the role she had to play. But John was clearly upset. Since he had to be home, he couldn't participate in after-school sports or join any clubs. Social get-togethers were likewise out of the question.

When he turned sixteen, John was given a car. At first, he was overjoyed with the generosity of his parents. But soon he learned that the car was to be used solely to get him rapidly home from school so he could tend to his mother, and his father could continue to work unabated.

Anger and Acting Out with Caregiving

John begged his parents to hire someone to play a caretaking role. He also thought that his sister could help more. But the parents reckoned she was too young and identified her as the "irresponsible" one. John was anointed the "family hero" and "savior."

So John was stuck in the thick of his mother's problem, and gradually his anger began to overwhelm him. His concentration suffered. His grades slid. The family reacted by becoming more and more demanding about his schoolwork. Meanwhile he thought, "What's the use? Even if I get into a good college, they'll never let me out of this snake pit. I'll be forced to attend the local junior college. It's unfair."

John's high school counselor summoned him because his grades had slipped so dramatically. John appeared to most of his teachers to be very distracted, and his counselor wanted to know what was going on. John couldn't contain the family fable any longer and disclosed to the counselor that he was caring for his mother for two to four hours a day and felt out of control. He wanted to oblige his father and help his mother. But the thought of being trapped in his house had become unbearable. He wanted to either get out of the circumstances or die—he told the counselor that sometimes he could taste the metal of a gun barrel in his mouth. Mostly though, he couldn't wait until he was old enough to leave home. As it happened, the counselor provided emotional support and academic guidance until John graduated. His father was too proud to keep John away from the college of his choice and so John was able to "escape" to college and experience personal freedom for the first time in years.

I saw John twenty years after the events described here. Like his father, he had become a successful physician. But he continued to harbor resentments over the caregiving role he had been forced to assume early in his life.

Comparing Janet and John

In both cases, the disordering of the usual parent and child roles added to the stress of each caretaker's situation. Children had to develop new roles with parental pressure but without parental guidance. In Dan's case, the caretaking authority was moved away from the parents and given to Janet. John lost respect for the authority of his mother and was angry for years over the demands that his father placed upon him. One reason he chose to see me was that he wanted to learn to forgive his father and to be sure that he never did this to any of his children.

Both these families also experienced problems with addressing feelings. Caregiving was needed that the designated caregiver did not want to provide, and the resulting anger was muffled or suffocated. As people begin to stifle their feelings, they begin to find ways to not experience the feelings. So they don't talk to or trust others, and they begin to feel shame. What the caregiver feels here is similar to what we call burnout in the work world. The next case explores caregiving burnout in a loving couple.

Meg's Case

Meg was in a relationship with Dave when she had her first panic attack. She was twenty-one. Dave was just finishing graduate school and was hoping to apply for a position at a large biotech company in the San Francisco Bay Area. He knew a lot about neuropsychological problems and thought that he would be able to research and help ease Meg's dilemma.

Dave was the poster boy of the willing caregiver. He had a warm personality, an interest in the science of the disorder, and the time to contribute. He sought out the best advice from the best clinicians, read everything there was to read on agoraphobia, and consulted with friends who knew something about the nuances of psychopharmacology. Dave truly loved Meg and wanted to help her. But he became tired from his superdemanding efforts. What he had not anticipated was that being a good caregiver and being someone who could successfully help Meg overcome agoraphobia were two different experiences.

After a while Dave began to capitulate to the anxieties Meg felt. She was willing to go out of the house, but she would only go in a particular direction and she was not willing to cross any bridges, however small. So Dave began to work out his routes beforehand. He also didn't want people to visit the home who might upset her. And he didn't want to pressure her to return to work even though they needed the money. His frustration and self-doubt grew as he continued to sacrifice and adjust, and Meg still didn't improve.

With agoraphobia, improvement is apparent: people are either doing better or they aren't. They're able to go outside or they're not. There isn't much of a gray area in terms of behavior, though some agoraphobics become able to go out from the home but are never comfortable with it. Others are able to recover completely, although they often fear a relapse.

Caregivers want their companions to get better. They want their own lives back, too. Like Dave, they may also want to share in the credit for the recovery. For all these reasons, a lack of improvement can be very discouraging to a companion who has given everything that she or he had.

The Impact on the Family

In cases like these, which I have seen over and over again, the impact of agoraphobia on the caregiver or concerned family members is readily apparent. Unlike many other psychiatric problems, agoraphobia has an unrelenting impact on the family. People who are psychotic or schizophrenic can be hospitalized or heavily medicated, and they can often live in shelters, halfway houses, or board and care homes, sometimes for the rest of their lives. But the agoraphobic doesn't experience much of a continuously apparent syndrome as long as he or she remains home and feels safe. There are certainly more than a few caregivers who don't have the freedom to say "no" to helping out. John didn't, and Dave didn't feel he did. Others have characterized themselves as wimps, expressing guilt that they feel unequal to the demands put on them. Janet, deeply conflicted about helping, felt that she never stuck up for herself. Thus the caregiver is in a type of jail, perhaps with more freedom to move than the agoraphobic, but confined nevertheless.

Agoraphobia and Work

Like Dan, an agoraphobic may be a little jumpy, but he or she can be a normal-functioning, productive, hardworking individual if put into the right environment. Agoraphobics are sometimes in professions where they work in their homes and have little or no contact with people. There are writers who are agoraphobic. Alex was able to work in a photographic darkroom in his home; the driver who picked up and delivered packages to his house was his only source of regular contact with others.

Other clients of mine have been able to work regularly as long as they worked at night and could get to and from work without any hassles and maintain a regimented routine. Similarly, a colleague of mine had a graphic-artist husband who could function quite well as long as he didn't travel any farther than five miles from his home or traverse any bridges.

There are other models of people who worked successfully in well-defined territories. The late and continuously popular cartoonist Charles Schulz was notorious for his variety of fears and foibles, according to people who knew him. But he managed to live comfortably and function with tremendous success by arranging his life so that there was little change in his daily routine. For example, he ate breakfast in the same restaurant at the same table for years. And the people around him grew to respect his privacy, which no doubt helped him maintain his equilibrium.

Caregiving and the Family System

To understand what is most upsetting to you as a caregiver, you need to consider life as a part of a system of relationships. In family systems, people assume certain roles based on their relationships, and the others expect them to display the accompanying behaviors. Parents, for example, are supposed to support the family unit, protect the children and the household, give instruction and guidance when it is necessary, and utilize authority when the situation calls for it. Regardless of age, children often expect that they can rely upon their parents, feel protected in their growth, and learn how to address the vicissitudes of life, so they can eventually realize their potential.

When the family structure is disrupted, caregiving can become even more difficult than it might otherwise be. In several of the family circumstances illustrated above there were a number of demanding characteristics: authority seemed to be absent or misplaced, and the children were left without healthy adult role models or a sense that their safety and growth mattered.

You can compare a family system to a mobile: the different parts are balanced evenly and can rotate around each other; when stirred, a mobile always returns to some state of equilibrium. But when it's unbalanced or constantly in a breeze, the mobile is never able to regain its harmony. That, I think, is a useful way to characterize the impact of agoraphobia in a family relationship.

In any relationship, patterns of behavior can be understood as an equation of actions, reactions, and interactions. Dan had a problem. He took action by asking for help from Janet. Janet reacted to the request. Her reaction set up a new, conflicted pattern of interaction between herself and Dan: he wanted her to give him more support than a sister usually does, and Janet wanted to assist only partially. So their action-reaction-interaction equation became more complex, and their old, familiar pattern of behavior changed.

On the family stage, there are a number of such relationships: there are mother-daughter, father-son, mother-son, father-daughter, sister-brother, and mother-father relationships that create any number of actual and potential interactions. So the system is very complex.

Society also places role definitions on the family. It's assumed that children's roles involve learning, growing, and feeling protected. They are to be attended to and given a strong degree of attention, support, and structure by the parents, who teach and guide and serve as role models. But if a parent becomes agoraphobic, roles become very confused. That's what John experienced.

A child who is witness to agoraphobia or is a caregiver for an agoraphobic has many of the same experiences as a child in an alcoholic family. The child is forced out of his or her appropriate role and is not able to have his or her needs met. The child must learn to stifle individual needs, to suppress real feelings.

These children are embarrassed by their parents. And since they're not receiving the habitual protection and reinforcement from their parents, they begin to experience life differently from their peers. They feel shame, loss, and pain. They learn to distrust the world; they begin to become numb to life events.

Family Therapy and Agoraphobia

Family therapists observe and intervene in situations where they perceive that the problem lies not in the individual but in the ways the family members communicate. Certainly family issues can be a part of the caregiving process and family therapy might be a consideration if the problems of both agoraphobia and the caregiving process impact the whole family.

One type of therapeutic perspective on the family suggests that the individual might have difficulty separating himself or herself from the family. From this perspective, one could argue that the agoraphobic really wants to remain a child and feels severe anxiety when confronted with the prospect of entering the adult world of work and relationships.

Another family systems perspective suggests that the family of an agoraphobic is enmeshed (that is, the members do not have healthy boundaries with one another), and that the agoraphobic really manifests a symptom of the family's underlying problems. If the agoraphobic has learned that "fearfulness" or "incompetence" is a role to play, then maybe he or she can play it better than the others in the family—think of Dan's role as the one doomed to fail. Conversely, very clever agoraphobes or other seemingly psychiatrically disabled people have been known to manipulate the family, perhaps unconsciously, by being absolutely unable to perform in a social world. It can be a way for such people to get what they want within the family. Therapists must be alert to such dynamics.

The next chapter will help you understand how you've initially handled the crisis of having an agoraphobic companion. It will also allow you to become a bit more conscious of the often dismaying thoughts, beliefs, and activities that may have become part of your routine.

2

How Are You Dealing with the Agoraphobia?

Let's be honest for a moment. You probably feel more frequently than you'd like to admit that you want to escape from this predicament. If you're like the other heavily involved family members that I've worked with, you probably hate to hear the phone ring when you're away from home or at work. You likely expect that it's your companion needing you to come home, or at the least, to pick up something from a store that's miles out of the way.

Unfortunately, you can't run away. But you can develop some mechanisms for coping with the life circumstance you're in. You'll need to gather some strength, much as a person needs to stay in the hospital for a while after a medical intervention. Step back. You don't want to put yourself in the position of continuing to create your own self-imposed prison. You're the same person you were before this crisis entered your life, and you can make adjustments that are more mindful and substantially less reactive than fleeing would be.

Remember, this experience may be different from other types of problems in your life, but your current way of handling it is probably similar to the ways you've handled other crises. That may need to change. For instance, if you've handled other major problems in your life by assuming control and doing it all yourself, you may become overwhelmed. Instead, try to break some of your caregiving activities into smaller steps to make them more manageable. You will also need to learn to delegate activities to other support people. So you'll need to give up some control. And, you need to affirm to yourself both that the task is difficult and that you can manage it. Is this caregiving responsibility colossal? Yes. Is it wrenching? Yes. Can you handle it? Yes, you can.

In Chapter 1 you were offered descriptions of different reactions people have when agoraphobia invades their lives. That was done to help you recall how you felt when this all started. Now you'll explore how caregiving is emotionally affecting you currently. In my experience talking to caregivers over the years, what I've learned to be most concerned about are not the facts of the situation they're in but rather the way they've reacted to them.

Do Others Know What You Feel?

As a caregiver, your companion and probably at least one other person close to both of you believe that you can cope with this. Try to take in some of that positive thinking, but don't feel you have to cope all alone. Others believe you have the strength—do you?

When my client Erin was asked to assist her mother, she thought there was no way she could take her mother to the store, drive her to her therapist, and ensure she had some visitors to the home other than herself. She resented the fact that no one else in the family, including her two older brothers, would help out.

Erin never asked for help; she never delegated. She just got mad. After a while she found that her energy level had depleted. She was emotionally drained and burned out; she had lost twelve pounds since she began caregiving. Angrily, she asked her oldest brother, Ray, why he never assisted or even volunteered to help. Ray responded that it just seemed like she enjoyed what she was doing, that she was closer to her mother than the boys, and that neither of them thought there was any problem to speak of.

Erin was shocked. But when she recalled how she had handled the problem, she had to reluctantly agree with her brother. She had never made any cry for help, and a part of her believed that she could handle most of this on her own. It was only when she began to regularly oversleep and lose weight that she realized she needed to call in the cavalry.

What Can You Do for Yourself?

You probably have friends who seem to handle large projects and major life crises with more ease than you do. And you probably admire them describing them as a "pillar of strength" or a "rock of Gibraltar." If you feel that applying such descriptions to yourself is laughable, let me suggest that you take a lesson from corporate executives.

Strategize, Consult, Execute

My experience in consulting with my career and business clients has taught me about what extraordinarily successful businesspeople are able to do in the presence of a crisis. First, they strategize quickly. Then they expand upon their strategic plan by consulting with trusted others. Thereafter, they execute the plan, knowing what to do themselves and what to delegate. But most importantly, they do all this calmly, with equanimity.

Now, I need to point out that it's the best managers who can do all this. If everyone were naturally able to handle crises like yours, there would be no need for this book—or maybe for any other self-help books for that matter. In reality, most people have to be taught and coached in these skills. So let's explore what people do when they respond to crises. Then let's compare that to what you did when the circumstances of your life changed because of agoraphobia.

Reactions to Crises

When Janet was first confronted with Dan's panic attacks, she also panicked. She spent most of her time first trying to ascertain her own role and then figuring out how to extricate herself from some of her involvement. Clearly she had an active emotional reaction. But she didn't engage in creative thinking about how to solve the immediate crisis. And she didn't plan to delegate responsibility in the future to keep from becoming overwhelmed.

When Dave first realized Meg had a problem, he wanted to do what it took to help her get better. But in so doing he became more like a whirling dervish than someone who could engage in strategic planning. In addition, he took all of the responsibility for Meg's needs on himself, so that he wasn't able to delegate.

Let's explore your initial reactions to your own crisis. Are you able to strategize, consult, and execute when you're under fire?

Your Initial Reactions

Explore what your initial emotional reactions were to learning that your loved one had a panic attack. You may do this by answering the following questions on a separate piece of paper:

- What did you feel when you were first asked to assist?

- Did you try to minimize the problem, or deny there was a problem? If you did, can you recall some of the unhelpful phrases you might have used? Were there any helpful phrases that you used that you may have forgotten about?

- Did you feel any sympathy? What were some of the sympathetic, or unsympathetic thoughts you remember having?

- How did you feel panic over your own life circumstances changing? Did you focus only or mostly upon your own plight?

- Did you believe initially that your companion was absolutely terrified? Why or why not?

- Did you feel protective of your companion? Do you feel now that you may have been even overly protective?

- Did you try to view the crisis from your companion's perspective or only from yours? If you found your life to be immediately disrupted, did you feel some degree of forgiveness for your companion?

The purpose of this exercise is twofold. First, it allows you to begin to scrutinize some of the self-defeating messages, emotions, or "baggage" that you carry within the caregiving predicament. It's this baggage that keeps you from being able to strategize, consult, and execute. Second, it allows you to explore for yourself whether or not you're able to experience your companion's point of view or experience. It inquires into whether your focus was primarily on yourself.

Other Points of View

People who are eminently successful at managing different crises simultaneously, whether in business or on the home front, are able to understand the points of view of all of the parties. What you may find from really listening to your companion and to your own fears and assumptions is that you have not understood other points of view. The ensuing chapters of this book will help you increase your knowledge about what is happening to your companion so your point of view can expand to include his or hers.

Good business managers consider all points of view in a crisis. If you're able to identify your point of view and see how it's different from that of your companion, you'll begin to understand your involvement. Furthermore, you can begin to understand the points of view of others in the family or other people to whom you may want to delegate some responsibility. This type of understanding can aid substantially in the recovery process for all of you.

Your Personal Issues with Becoming a Caregiver

You've undoubtedly asked yourself many times how you happened into the caregiving role. Use the following checklist to clarify your feelings. Grasping some of the personal issues that you have about this role can make you more sensitive to the point of view of your companion.

Checklist: Assuming the Caretaker Role

Check all of the issues that you believe are reasons you have the companion role to an agoraphobic:

_____ I got into this relationship for better or worse.

_____ I have unusual compassion for my companion.

_____ I feel guilty in that for some reason I'm partially to blame for this.

_____ I feel that I am being manipulated and controlled by someone else.

_____ I am familiar with playing the role of the victim.

_____ I feel that if I don't do this, the family will fall apart.

_____ I feel that my companion will be unable to exist without me.

_____ No one else in my family or network seems to be able to do anything.

_____ No one else in my family or network seems to be willing to do anything.

_____ I was asked to take on this role.

_____ The family has always been dysfunctional; maybe I can make it right.

_____ I have been frightened before and I know how to help frightened people.

_____ I have had my own panic attacks and panic disorder in the past, so I know best how to help.

_____ I tend to get myself into dysfunctional relationships.

_____ An authority figure (like a parent) asked me to do this.

_____ I've been abused by a family member and I think abuse caused my companion to have this problem.

_____ People in my family are verbally aggressive and I think that caused the problem. I am quiet and know how to help.

_____ I don't feel there are any boundaries between me and my agoraphobic companion. What my companion feels, I feel.

_____ I have a tendency to overextend myself.

Interpreting the Checklist

I have developed this checklist over the years. The items reflect reasons given by family members when asked why they were trying so diligently to assist their psychiatrically disabled companions.

Look back over the checklist. What do you learn about yourself? Are you contributing your time and effort of your own free will? Or do you feel as if you're being coerced into doing something that doesn't feel so very good? These are probably tough questions to ask yourself, but this kind of query is important.

Some of your own rational decision making could be impaired by your taking on the role that you have. You might feel that you defend yourself when others ask simple questions about your role. Or you might wish that someone else would help you, but you haven't a clue about how to ask. Remember that very good managers know what and when they should delegate to others. But keep in mind that in order to delegate, you have to believe that others are capable of assisting. You also have to be willing to share the responsibilities and to relinquish the feeling that you need to control the entire situation.

People do indeed like to help. My own counseling colleagues—caregivers and health and mental health professionals—often get involved in the business of helping and healing others because they've had experiences that make them uniquely qualified to help. Moreover, in the counseling department at San Francisco State University, the faculty always takes note of the number of students who choose to enter our program because of their own positive experiences with a disabled family member. Others are simply empathic, and can't stand to see a loved one in psychological pain.

Some are caregivers because of the unfolding of their own problems and issues. They may be in codependent relationships with their companions. They may have an insurmountable need to control another person's behavior. Or they may need someone else to have a certain degree of control over their own behavior. Similarly, some caregivers feel that if they tie themselves to people who are overly dependent, they will not be lonely.

Your Own Reactions

Not only do you need to consider your perspective, but you also need to explore your own reactions to crises. Contemplating how you handle other troublesome situations in your life is useful in understanding how you're handling this one. Try to candidly judge past crises. Do you usually respond with a panicky and hysterical reaction? If that's the case, embarrassing as it may seem, then it's likely that you have responded to this crisis with your companion no differently. With this realization you begin to acknowledge those situations that are terribly threatening to you and the sense of order in your life.

Analyzing Your Fears and Panicky Reactions

Let's consider your reactions to stressful and threatening events by examining four different arenas: your body reactions, the personal messages that you give yourself, your behavior under stress, and your overall interpretation of these three reactions. I have used this method in working with individuals who have been fired from a job or are unable to secure a position (Chope 2000).

Go back to the events that brought you to caring for an agoraphobic companion. You'll be listing the reactions you had when you first heard the cry for help. If you need to, close your eyes and reflect upon that initial experience, hearing what was said and remembering what you did. Try to be as honest and thorough as you can.

1. First, identify reactions that took place in your body, even if it was something as simple as getting stomach cramps or "butterflies." Do you remember any changes in your muscles or in your breathing? Did your heart appear to beat more quickly or to have a pounding feeling?

2. Now write down what messages you gave yourself in response to these events. For example, did you say things like "I can't handle this," "I already have too much in my life to deal with," "This isn't fair," "Who's going to care for me?" These "poor me" types of messages are often heard from caregivers who feel panic and immense frustration when they're called upon to handle a crisis.

3. For the third part of the exercise, try to remember what behaviors you engaged in when you realized that you were going to be called upon to help. If you had a "poor me" reaction, did you then say something like, "Poor me. Poor me. Pour me another drink" (that is, did you try to escape responsibility by using drugs or alcohol)? Did you run toward the situation to give a hand? Did you try to avoid being involved by running away or not answering the phone? Did you reach out and call upon others for help?

4. Finally, how did you interpret the life changes that were occurring? Did you tell yourself that there is very little you can't handle? Did you feel like you wanted to captain the family ship? Or did you feel that this was absolutely overwhelming and that your own life was spinning out of control?

Now use this process to recall a more recent life crisis that you had strong reactions to. This could be something like a confrontation with a boss or a significant other, the aftermath of a car accident, or the loss of a valuable item. Reflect upon how you handled this crisis, taking yourself through the same four steps of the exercise.

These activities assist you in understanding how you manage crises. Understanding what your own reaction is means you'll be better able to modify it to be more appropriate. If you need to adjust some of your reactions, knowing what happens in your body, in your head, and in your behavior is the best possible preparation. This is referred to as "shifting your point of view" or "reframing" the situation you're in. Being able to shift like this can beef up your effectiveness as a caregiver. Understanding how you react to different crises can also help you to learn to anticipate how you're going to handle a new situation.

Did You Plan to Fix This Right Away?

Many managers who fail are those whose response to a crisis is immediate, impulsive, and unorganized. It's important for you to explore your willingness to strategize, consult, and execute in developing a long-term program for yourself and your agoraphobic companion. Though we live in a world where everyone expects everything to be completed yesterday, try to avoid that mentality. It puts too much pressure on both of you.

As I indicated in the Introduction, most of the caregivers who refer agoraphobics to me seem to have several things in common. They bring an overwhelming amount of energy to the table, and they seem to have already developed their own treatment blueprint and a time line. They often appear to be looking for some sort of validation from me for their plan, as well as help implementing it. They're often taken aback when I make statements about the complexities of agoraphobia and its unpredictability with regard to results, and when I say I would like the treatment plan to involve the other family members.

Certainly this approach puts many people off. But it does slow the process down a bit and get everyone conceptualizing a strategy that will help both the agoraphobe and the caregivers. I want to foster consultation, team building, and execution.

Although it may feel to the agoraphobe like too much pressure, I think it's useful for caregivers to consider, together with their companions, a possible deadline for the completion of a strategy. What outcome does the agoraphobic desire? Do they want to be able to go to work? Go to the store? Go out of the house? Do they want intense therapeutic work initially with a tapering off, or steady treatment over a period of time? Involving the entire family in the process, I develop a "reverse calendar" to fit the types of strategies that might work within certain time lines. I find that developing a strategy with time constraints can give the entire family useful indicators. You might consider using a seasoned therapist to assist with the planning process. However you make your plans, it's essential that you aid and discuss everyone's expectations of the recovery process, so it doesn't engender added frustration and feelings of pressure.

Organize Your Helping Activities

When crises emerge, people often try to handle all aspects of the crisis at once rather than planning what to do (strategizing, consulting, executing). But to help prevent any further crises in your caregiving, try to spend time each day planning. Self-help groups and religious organizations suggest you begin the day repeating affirmations, focusing on goals, or using a reader like the Daily Word. This ritual enforces a few brief, balanced, and peaceful goals for yourself.

If you're unable to do this, at least give yourself some time at the beginning of each day in your own comfortable place (whether it's in your home, office, or neighborhood) and visualize where you hope to be at different times during the day. This practice can help you take some degree of control over your attempts at accomplishing different goals throughout the day.

Whatever the ritual you choose, the more it becomes commonplace to your life, the more it will serve to support you.

Refrain from Worry

If the circumstances you're in seem to be causing you unnecessary worry, it's time to try to get a degree of control over that. Ed Hallowell (1997) suggests a number of different techniques for dealing with worry. The first is to separate out good worry from bad worry. He suggests that good (or realistic) worrying is a type of planning. So continue with it. He's more concerned about "toxic worry," the worry that is fed by unproductive, excessive, repetitive thoughts that come out of nowhere, and are of no real consequence. I characterize these as "what if" worries: "What if my companion doesn't get better?" "What if my companion can never work again?" "What if my companion will never be able to travel or to go to social gatherings again?" There's not much productive about this; in fact, "what if" worries can be completely debilitating

If you have to worry, try some creative maneuvers. Try to worry in the same place each day, even if it means creating a worry room. Hallowell suggests that you not worry alone. Worrying with someone means that your worries and those of another can be given some sort of validation.

Other activities work, too. Try to get the facts about agoraphobia. (The next chapter of this book will help.) Consult an expert and use real-life or online support groups like those listed at the end of the book. Information will definitely serve as some type of support.

Freeing yourself from unnecessary worry will allow you to become much more optimistic, pleasant to be around, and energetic.

Focus Your Tasks

As you go through your day, try to attend to the activities that you've planned. Check in with yourself during quiet moments: Where are you in relation to the plans that you have set for yourself? How many have been accomplished, how many are a work in progress, and how many are yet to be done?

If you can stay on task in the midst of the change and turmoil in your life you're already starting to get some control over the effects the agoraphobia has on you. As you complete each of the tasks you've set for yourself, be sure to give yourself some recognition. Completing will definitely give you some feeling of your own accomplishments.

Planning for Stress

Workshops, groups, and lectures on stress are everywhere. This is probably because stress is essentially inescapable. Research has shown that the simple changing of life through different events, whether positive or negative, can produce experiences that are characterized as stressful (Holmes and Rahe 1967).

When you begin to care for your agoraphobic companion, you move into essentially uncharted territory. (And unlike a lot of other life events, this one does not include either a choice or a rite of passage. It was simply thrust upon you.) With the changes you're experiencing, you need to develop new and probably very different coping skills. Learning how to identify your feelings in the face of life events, acknowledging and recording the activities you engaged in while caring for your companion, and educating yourself about the alternative ways of handling your companion's problems are all useful activities. Knowing how to strategize, consult, and execute will help, too.

Stress is often the variable that brings out the very worst in people, so if you're feeling under inordinate stress, you may not be the best and most effective caregiver that you can be. Most people feel stress in their work life; if you're in a stressful workplace and you don't respond well to either work-related stress or the stress of caregiving, you may have a real problem keeping yourself functioning productively.

You may have already developed your own buffers to the stress of caregiving. You may also feel that you're in a very loving relationship with your companion. But it's still useful to keep note of the interactions that you're having with your companion, including the types of conflicts that seem to be the most aggravating.

The brief assessment that follows can give you a sense of how much the stress of this condition is affecting you and whether you should develop a program of stress reduction activities.

Do You Need a Stress Inoculation?

Read the following questions and determine whether or not any of them apply to you.

1. Have you had any major physical illnesses since you began caring for your companion? This could include a prolonged influenza, stomach cramps, heartburn, and rashes like neurodermatitis.

2. Have you become more argumentative with the people around you, like your friends, coworkers, and other family members?

3. Do you often go to bed saying that you have taken on more than you can handle? (You might consider whether this is a typical pattern in your life. If it is, then caring for your companion is probably not the root cause of the feeling.).

4. Do you find you have a difficult time experiencing anything that's very pleasurable? Do you find too that you don't treat yourself to many special events? Do you think that you may use your companion as an excuse for this?

5. Do you now have a tendency to think that events aren't going to turn out very well for you and your companion? Is this a new feeling that has emerged since the agoraphobia appeared?

6. Do you regularly have negative thoughts about yourself?

7. Do you find that you're demanding more attention or bragging about yourself more than you used to?

8. Do you feel like you're constantly in a hurry?

9. Have you found that you've increased your use of substances like drugs and alcohol since you began caregiving?

If you answered "yes" to any of the questions listed here, then you are probably a good candidate for some stress reducing activities. Later chapters of this book contain a variety of such activities for your companion; try these yourself to gain some emotional control over your caregiving experience.

Caregiving Can Add Meaning to Life

Some people not only adapt to the caregiving experience but may even achieve a new sense of identity and purpose by having it. In a few ways, caregivng is not unlike being a therapist. Psychotherapeutic work can be filled with so much pressure, and at times it's difficult to listen to problems all day. There are times when even well-trained and highly experienced therapists feel vulnerable, just like caregivers. Still, many of us enter this business because of a fascination for human problems and the meaning they give to life.

Areas of Vulnerability

There are probably a variety of ways you're feeling particularly vulnerable or inadequate. See if any of the following scenarios apply to you.

Self-Doubt

You probably feel you don't have the skills for this. Maybe you feel you're too young, too old, or too inexperienced or that you simply have no idea what to do. It's very important for you to feel that you don't have to be an expert in everything you do as a caregiver.

Try to eliminate words like "could" and "would" and especially "should" from your vocabulary. As you learn new caregiving skills, allow yourself to say to yourself, to your companion, and to others that you're just learning how to do this. If a new therapeutic technique or drug appears on the market, try to learn as much about it as you have time for, but don't put the demand on yourself to be an expert on new pharmaceuticals.

If you have a tendency to remember what you don't do rather than what you do, you might try keeping a written record of your successes as a caregiver. You don't have to share this with anyone else, but if you choose, you might consider showing it to your own therapist or another person who can give you some encouragement.

But a written record of your accomplishments can go a long way toward bolstering your self-esteem. Try to include all of your accomplishments, even if they involve a degree of drudgery.

Janet kept a regular journal of her caregiving activities. In doing so, she found that she no longer needed to defend herself to the family or to Dan because she was fully aware of what she had contributed. Interestingly, she discovered in the process that what most people, including Dan, appreciated was something she might not have given herself credit for. Others most appreciated her willingness to provide a lot of the transportation in the early stages of Dan's agoraphobia.

Role Reversal

If you're serving your family in some caregiving capacity, you may be in the middle of an unfamiliar role reversal. Our aging population has many examples of couples who have to change roles in order to care for each other. Older men who become caregivers may have to learn to cook for the first time, while older women caregivers may find they're physically stronger than their ailing husbands, and that it's up to them to do some of the "heavier lifting." Janet, who used to have a rivalry with her brother Dan, was now in the position of providing care and fostering communication.

Changing roles with someone can result in the shattering of illusions. You may find it's terribly difficult to see that a parent you once viewed as so strong is now weak. Meg was aware of her own mother's weakness at an early point in her life. She recalled that her mother was unable to sit anywhere in her church except in the back pew. When her mother was asked by a friend to participate in a wedding as the matron of honor, she was able to participate only if Meg were assigned an aisle seat during the ceremony. Meg found this experience to be emotionally demanding, and for the first time she had to act toward her mother in an unfamiliar manner.

In a relationship, one or the other person may engage in undesirable behaviors and quirks, and these can become more noticeable and vexing during the caregiving process. Both the caregiver and the agoraphobe will need to ask each other for a little more patience and flexibility with these quirks as you adjust to the changes in your relationship.

Communication Problems

One function of a caregiver is to tell others how the agoraphobe is doing. This is not always easy. You want to give other family

members proper information, but you also want them to be respon-
sive to you if you need help. In some ways, you're the most powerful
person in the family, even if you don't feel that way. Janet found
family communication difficult when she was trying to assist Dan.
When she called with a brief report, her parents would grill her,
demanding the most miniscule of details. She often phoned after
work and was frankly exhausted after these difficult calls.

Like many other caregivers I've talked with, Janet also found it
was very difficult to ask for help from the family. This task becomes
complicated when you simultaneously cry for some assistance and
report information. People often want the information, but they
don't want to be asked to help. As a caregiver you may find it's most
effective to ask for assistance at times when you're not recounting
information. It may also become important for you to set limits on
the time and energy you spend reporting information.

Perhaps the best way to negotiate reinforcement from the other
members of the family is to set a schedule of your activities and
inform others when you will not be available. With this schedule in
mind, others can make some choices about how and when they can
serve which will in turn make it likelier that you'll get the help you
need. The onus is still on you to keep them informed, but you all
must try to keep the relationships you've honed over the years
intact. They're a big investment.

When you communicate with your companion about caregiving
issues, try to keep your conversations as positive and productive as
you can. Try to set certain times during the day to talk together. Try
also to listen carefully to what your companion has to say about his
or her ups and downs, successes and failures.

Sometimes focusing on the problems makes it difficult to maintain aspects of the relationship that can be quite enjoyable. For example, if your companion is a spouse or a lover, you want to continue
to nurture your sexual attraction for each other. Counseling may be
of help here: when I worked with Meg, I also wanted work with
Dave to help him continue to view Meg as a love object and someone
he could have fun with, even if it was always at home.

Fear of Rejection

You may also feel there's quite an opportunity for rejection
here. No matter how hard you try or how much good work you
do, you probably won't satisfy all the family members or your
companion (or yourself) all of the time. You'll always be in the
position of having to say "no" or feeling you're coming up short in
some way.

Further, you may even feel you're in some sort of competition with others in your family. This may cause you to value your work and your opinions in terms of whether they are accepted or not. But this isn't a contest. In the long run, you are not going to remember much about which of your ideas were accepted and which weren't.

Some of your work will come down to achieving a degree of balance between what you want to offer and what works. It's important that you feel you have made your contribution; it's also important to hear others' suggestions, even though they may not ultimately lead to a positive outcome. Above all, you want to avoid feeling helpless, which will happen if you allow the rejection or criticism of others to get through to you.

Even though I worked with John twenty years after he had provided care to his mother, he continued to have resentments. Most of these were due to the rejection he felt he had received from both of his parents. In a general sense, he felt he had lost his childhood by caring for his mother. To him, that was the ultimate rejection of love.

John also felt that he was criticized regularly for what he hadn't done. He remembers that his father always had additional tasks for him, whether in running the house or caring for his mother. It was like he was never able to do enough, and he felt he received no recognition or reward for what he did do.

John felt that his mother also contributed to his feeling constantly criticized. When he arrived home from school, the house always had a peculiar odor, like there was nothing clean about it. John's mother chain-smoked, so there was always the smell of burnt tobacco around and the ashtrays were always full. He was expected to clean the ashtrays, straighten the house, start the oven for dinner, and make sure that his mother was comfortable.

A truly sad legacy for John is that he couldn't recall any of the good times in his upbringing. I remember asking him about vacations. Since his mother was unable to travel, the family didn't get away. John's only break was to attend summer camp for a week or two. Quite simply, he felt he never received the emotional sustenance that other boys his age did.

Distorted Thinking

Depending upon how your relationship to caregiving has gone in the past, there are probably some old messages that loom over you. Certainly John had held onto a number of these, including "I didn't do enough." It took a substantial amount of work reframing his childhood experiences for him to come to terms with how he had felt about himself.

Some aspects of your caregiving relationship will be demanding. But it's important that you don't hang onto outdated or distorted thinking. These distortions can affect your experience of working with your companion.

Probably one of the first messages you learned is that life can be very unpredictable. Well, that's for sure. But just because it's unpredictable doesn't mean that you can't also do some of your own planning. You probably also carry around the message that life is quite a struggle. (We've all heard the truism that "life is hard and then you die"). And what about the internal message you may accept as a truism, "I'm really not worth very much, am I?" Are there other unhelpful messages you carry? You might want to consider how you ended up with such "truisms" and how you have allowed them to influence your life.

With this in mind, use the following exercises to help understand your perceptions of who you are and how these perceptions may have been influenced by your family or your companion.

Perceptions of You and Your Caregiving

Write your answers to these questions on separate paper.

1. How have you been perceived by your companion at different stages of your relationship (beginning, middle, now)? What hard evidence do you have for this?

2. How have others, including your family, perceived you? What evidence do you have for this?

3. How have you perceived yourself in each stage?

Now, what can you recall about how these messages have influenced you? What do you recall about some of the old messages that have been given to you? Try these questions to jump-start your thinking:

1. Do you find yourself jumping to conclusions without hard evidence?

2. Do you see your efforts in your work in terms of an all-or-nothing experience? That is, you're either successful or you're not; there's no middle ground.

3. Do you obsess about details? Do you try to keep all of your bases covered?

4. Do you assume that the worst possible thing can happen, regardless of what you do?

This exercise will help you form accurate conclusions about your role. Let the data demonstrate your worthiness when you are confronting any intrusive, critical messages.

Resistance to Change

If you're like a lot of people, you probably don't want to change. Most of us tend to stay in situations that are familiar, even if they are uncomfortable. This is the reason people vacation in the same spots, stay in unhealthy relationships, and eat at the same restaurants (Chope 2000).

Life changes are inevitable. It's just that we all want to have more control over them than we do. In your present circumstances, you need to be willing to give up your belief that you can control the events around you. As I'll remind you throughout the book, you're in the middle of a real adventure; this is not a dress rehearsal.

As you react to changes that are out of your control, you may try to resist other, necessary changes that *are* in your control. You may not want to change your lifestyle, for example, or the ways you relate to your companion. Sylvia and her mother suffered from such stubborn resistance.

Sylvia cared for her aging, agoraphobic mother, who had high blood pressure and was terribly overweight, but who was not willing to make the lifestyle changes necessary to improve her health. Any attempt Sylvia made to change what her mother ate or how she lived ended up in a fight. Sylvia said it was just easier to let her mother eat inappropriate foods; to do otherwise would cause a rift in the relationship. Sylvia already felt that she had taken on more than enough responsibility and that the added burden of confronting her mother was simply too much for her.

Sylvia's mother needed to change her habits to improve her health. If Sylvia wanted to help her mother make this change, she in turn would have to change the way she related to her mother. She would have to calmly, firmly, and consistently confront her mother about her diet and lifestyle, perhaps enlisting the help of a doctor and other healthcare workers. The alternative, of course, would be for her to stop trying to control her mother's diet at all. Neither would be an easy choice, but some change was necessary if these two were to have a healthy relationship.

Understanding Personality Clashes

People in any relationship are going to have conflicts. That will be true in your love relationships, in your family, among your coworkers, with your boss, and amid people in your neighborhood, clubs, and spiritual gathering place.

When your caregiving became a larger part of your life, you and your family and your companion all brought your emotional baggage and unmet needs with you. Now more than ever, it's a good time to step back and take some stock of the kind of person you think you are in a relationship. Try this exercise, which I usually use with executives to assess their interpersonal workplace problems.

How Do Others View You?

Think of the people who are closest to you in your everyday life: coworkers, employees, siblings, parents, friends, and lovers. If each of these people were not talking to you, but instead were talking to their therapist about you, what do you think that they would say about how you function interpersonally? Would they say that you:

1. Are open to suggestions and criticism, or that you tend to stonewall others who disagree with you?

2. Tend to blame others for the problems that you're having?

3. Assume that everyone is just like you and that they ought to respond to crisis situations just like you?

4. Make people and their ideas seem important?

5. Tend to put time pressures and deadlines onto other people?

6. View those who are close to you as incompetent and/or get into regular debates with them?

7. Are someone people want to gravitate toward, or someone they try to avoid?

8. Feel that you need to be at the center of all of the decision making of the people around you? Like to do all of the event planning, make decisions on travel, and decide which movies to go to?

9. Are you seen as someone who is generous, or as someone with whom people do not want to make financial plans?

10. Have been able to cultivate long-term relationships with people, or are most of your relationships, including your work relationships, short-lived?

This exercise should help you understand some of the thornier aspects of your personality, especially those that can hinder your effectiveness as a caregiver. Simple differences of opinion can turn out to be almost incendiary given the histories and past circumstances of the parties in disagreement. The better you understand how you tend to deal with relationship issues, the less likely you are to start a major conflagration.

As you focus upon your interpersonal relationship with your companion:

- Try to have your own need to look good take a back seat.

- Try not to misread or misinterpret your companion's statements.

- Remember that even though at times you may feel like the person who is imprisoned, your companion feels the greatest degree of disempowerment.

What Kind of Social Skills Do You Have?

In your caregiving you're probably going to participate in meetings where complex medical and psychological information is discussed. You'll be exchanging information with others, including your family (or your companion's family) and your companion's psychological or medical care providers. This web of relationships will demand some social skills, including the ability to gather and disseminate information without constricting other helpers.

My client John recalled how poorly his family listened to the people who were trying to help his mother. He said it has taken years for him to realize how his father's own narcissism regarding his professional medical knowledge made it very difficult for him to let others be part of the caregiving process. John recalled how his father would assume the role of caregiver when there needed to be some sort of medical intervention. Later, he would criticize the people who were trying the most to help. John remembers his father scribbling notes when talking to his mother's psychiatrist. He often thought that his father preferred to be in some sort of a dispute with the psychiatrist than to create a positive accord. John referred to the family meetings held after his mother's providers left as the "monthly bloodletting."

Part of John's anger toward his father grew because his father never acknowledged John himself for his efforts or the results. Some of John's own depression and adolescent maladjustment was fed by this lack of recognition. Later, in his work with me, John began to realize that as bright and accomplished as his father was, his social skills were lacking. His father was a terrific communicator when he was in control. But when he had to relinquish that control to others, he was a terrible listener or talker.

How Empathic Are You?

How empathic are you toward your companion? You may have the best of intentions for your companion, and you are surely doing the very best you can. But it's also probable that in some way you feel a bit victimized by the circumstances you're in. That's certainly understandable. But if you are able to comfort and to soothe yourself, even when you feel victimized, you will likely be able to comfort and be empathic toward your companion.

However, if you tend to look to external sources for your own comfort, you may not have some of the internal resources necessary to behave empathically. For example, if in the course of your time as a caregiver you've comforted yourself with spending sprees, overeating, drinking excessive amounts of alcohol, using illegal or legal drugs and medications, or acting out in sexually inappropriate ways, then you have some evidence that your internal resources may be lacking.

Ideally, you're able to do what you're doing because you feel intimate with or connected to your companion. If you're feeling degraded or disempowered by the circumstances of being a caregiver, the chances of your being empathic remain small.

Malingering

According to the DSM-IV-TR *malingering* is the "intentional production of false or grossly exaggerated physical or psychological symptoms, motivated by external incentives such as avoiding military duty, avoiding work, obtaining financial compensation, evading criminal prosecution, or obtaining drugs." You may want to explore whether or not you feel your companion is malingering. If you feel this way, you might think it's your fault or that you're a less than stellar caregiver. Still, many caregivers feel from time to time that their agoraphobic companions could get better if they "would just try." In part, this belief comes from the fact that the companion, while in the home, seems to be symptom-free. Also, agoraphobia is complex and, difficult for someone who has never experienced a panic attack to understand.

Even the best caregivers I've worked with have felt from time to time that their companions were malingering, mostly because they didn't wish to return to work. When Dan's sister, Janet, became a caregiver, she was suspicious from the beginning that Dan wanted to be a little boy and really created his agoraphobia to avoid going to work.

If you want a quick way to discern whether your companion is a malingerer, look at the effort he or she is putting out, particularly in complying with the prescribed treatment regimen of a mental healthcare provider. Or you may want to note how willing your companion is to practice the exercises in later chapters of this book. If he or she resists the healing process, and you're convinced that you're as empathic as you can be, you may have some evidence for malingering. But rather than making your own diagnosis, consult with your companion's mental health professional.

Keep in mind that according to the DSM-IV-TR, malingering requires an external incentive for "symptom production." I've dealt with malingering on several occasions when individuals did not wish to return to work because they had a work-related problem. In one case, Will had a severe conflict with a boss; in another, Louise was forced to engage in behavior that was illegal and harassing. They both had good jobs, so it was difficult for family members to understand why they wouldn't return to work.

In my work with court-related referrals, I've happened upon clients for psychological testing and assessment who were trying to be declared permanently disabled. In a number of these cases, there were marked discrepancies between the client's alleged disability and my findings, and it wasn't difficult to make a diagnosis of malingering.

Factitious Disorders

There are also mental disorders in the DSM-IV-TR that can be characterized by physical or psychological symptoms that are "intentionally produced or feigned in order to produce the sick role." These are called *factitious disorders*, and they differ from malingering because there's no obviously recognizable goal. In a factitious disorder, "the motivation is a psychological need to assume the sick role, as evidenced by an absence of external incentives for the behavior."

In all of my experience, I've never encountered a client who had agoraphobic symptoms but was in fact suffering from a factitious disorder. Chances are very good that your companion doesn't have a factitious disorder. Still, you may want to be assured that this is the case by both your mental healthcare provider and your companion. You can sometimes tell that a person suffers from a factitious disorder if they present "their history with dramatic flair, but are extremely vague and inconsistent when questioned in greater detail" (513). People with factitious disorders are also grand complainers; those who have visited a hospital for treatment of a physical ailment typically use some sort of painkiller on a regular basis.

Empathic Understanding

Your empathy may be one of the most important ingredients in your caregiving. If you're able to view your companion with empathy, you probably have your own upbringing to thank. In a theory of personality development known as "object relations theory," having had loving and caring parental figures can allow you to do for others that which was done for you. Horner (1986) describes this as "having a loving mother within the self" (89). Your capacity to feel empathy suggests that you've been given inner resources and integrity that have come from a supportive and caring environment. Knowing this can help you to confront some of the frustration and despair that can come from your caregiving role.

Maintaining Boundaries

Hard as it may seem, part of your work in giving care is to maintain distance while at the same time being intimate—that is, to maintain appropriate boundaries. This probably sounds paradoxical, but it's an essential ingredient in the caregiving process, and it's the paradox that you (along with most therapists) must live with. The issue of boundaries will reemerge in later chapters. But for now, as you evaluate your relationship to your companion, consider whether you feel your identity is separate from your companion's and whether your worth as a person is predicated upon meeting your companion's needs. A separate identity and an independent sense of self-worth are essential components of good boundaries.

When John shared different remembrances of caring for his mother, he focused not just upon role issues but also on the ways she violated his boundaries. While he was fully prepared to help her with many of the exigencies of daily living, he found it very difficult to say "no" to her and he did not feel it was appropriate to spend as much time as he did ministering to her in her bedroom, in her bed-clothes. He felt that his mother had crossed the line between what was appropriate and what was not. Furthermore, he felt that his father had not protected him from a number of such uncomfortable encounters, and he harbored resentment toward his father for that.

Your Beliefs

Your beliefs are very potent in determining the kinds of decisions that you make in the caregiving role. In fact, there will be times when you make decisions based upon your beliefs, regardless of the information at hand. Beliefs can be:

1. Global or specific

2. Long-term propositions or rapidly changing

3. Rational or irrational

4. Productive or counterproductive

5. About you and about your companion

Your Beliefs about Your Role as a Caregiver

Using the five categories of beliefs listed above, list the beliefs you have about agoraphobia and about your role as a caregiver. You might want to divide a piece of paper into two sides, then list the beliefs against each other. You may set up your columns as follows:

1. Global beliefs   Specific beliefs

2. Long-term beliefs   Short-term beliefs

3. Rational beliefs   Irrational beliefs

4. Productive beliefs   Counterproductive beliefs

5. Beliefs about me   Beliefs about my companion

What you write will be a sort of summary statement about your beliefs. Don't judge the beliefs, just allow them to help you understand where you're coming from. If there's a belief that your companion should try harder, get better sooner, or is faking it, then record it.

A source for understanding more about the complexity of beliefs is Robert Kegan's book *In Over Our Heads* (1994). Kegan sees the creation of beliefs as a way of understanding who we are personally, culturally, and socially. He says that through our beliefs, we're all builders of what he refers to as "meaning-making" in our lives. Making meaning of your life from your beliefs about caregiving will allow you to become more tolerant of ambiguity and less self-critical of your role as a caregiver.

Confronting Unhelpful Beliefs

You want to use your beliefs to create an improved caregiving process. More, you want to also be able to regularly prevent counterproductive beliefs, such as those described in the next paragraphs.

"This Situation Is Hopeless"

This is the most common complaint I hear from people, and it really doesn't do anyone any good. It ends up in angst, depression, or paralysis. If you have hopelessness in your belief system, you need to look at how you constructed this belief, what you receive emotionally from the belief, how the belief influences your behavior, and how it reflects who you are as a human being.

In my experience, I've found that those who call themselves hopeless or believe everything is hopeless are trying to eliminate some feelings of oppression. If everything is hopeless, then they don't have to do very much, since not much of what they are going to do is going to be very useful. If hopelessness is your belief, your work is to put meaning into the caregiving process. Presumably, this book is already assisting you with this.

You can also try to start disputing some of your "hopeless" beliefs. Martin Seligman, former president of the American Psychological Association, believes we need to develop a more upbeat and positive psychology. Learning how to confront dysfunctional and counterproductive beliefs is a step in the direction of creating this more positive psychology in yourself.

"I'm Helpless"

I've always appreciated the irony that most people who have this belief have been utterly successful in their lives. What most "helpless" people have experienced is a great deal of confidence in other parts of their lives. Now, they're confronted with something they may not be very good at, which is really inconsistent with who they think they are in the world.

The work for "I'm helpless" persons is to apply strategies of behavior from the other parts of their lives to the area of caregiver, engaging in at least one productive behavior each day. This practice will get you beyond the feeling of being helpless.

"This Is Too Intrusive"

That's undoubtedly correct. But so are a lot of the other annoyances of life. There are always going to be intrusions. Your work is to be able to bounce back from the intrusions. The difference between the intrusion of agoraphobia and, say, the theft of your car is that you know how to deal with a car theft, but it's much more difficult to know what to do with the mental disorder of someone you love.

Flexibility and Rigidity

Since you're assisting with the mental health needs of someone else, you're not always going to get your way, and your companions are not always going to engage in the behaviors that you want them to. In my lectures about mental health, I've often told my students that I could sum up mental health in one word: "flexibility." As a caregiver, you'll find that more than anything else you do, you'll be most appreciated for your flexibility—your generous, nonjudging encouragement and support.

You may need to be most flexible if your companion relapses after showing immense improvement. People relapse, and it's not necessarily anyone's fault. So don't adversely judge yourself or your companion if this takes place.

Embrace Change

Your caregiving work is going to demand that you embrace change. You'll need to give up on the notion of having any certainty in this process. You'll be required to accept some aspects of your companion's behavior that will be disheartening. The way you define success may need retooling. The path you're on now is going to take you two steps forward and a step back—and there might even be an excursion off the path or a fall down a canyon.

You're going to need to create new partnerships with other caregivers, support groups, and other resources in the community. You may have to bond with other family members, or your companion's family members even when you don't care for them. You're not going to necessarily change the people and the institutions around you, but you can be willing to change your attitudes about them.

There are more and more interesting resources available. Your work is going to be in sorting and evaluating them. You'll be at your best with a certain degree of flexibility.

Give Up Control

If you're feeling you've failed, it may be an indication that you're not being flexible enough with yourself. Accept that failure with one strategy means simply that you'll need to try something else. The key here is to not create a mental atmosphere that screams "failure."

Also, if you're putting the failure label on yourself, then you may be doing it to your companion. If that's the case, you are making your companion and yourself performers, rather than individuals who are addressing mental health concerns. In almost all cases, successes come after significant failures. Try to see any of your failures or your companion's as behaviors that are moving you ahead.

Everything that you're addressing now with your companion is uncertain and that's something that you're just going to have to get used to. You're not going to be able to control any events, your companion's activities or wishes, or the opinions of the professionals you've chosen to include in this experience.

Almost certainly, most of what you're fearful of is losing control. Let's be real. The only thing you can control is your own behavior. Most people don't want to lose control. So they engage in activities that presume that they have some control. Julia Sweeney's play, *God Said, "Ha!"* (which is now out on video), is a wonderful, comical illustration of how she and her family coped with her brother's diagnosis of cancer. This one-woman show describes with allegorical detail the reality that none of us has much control. It also has brilliant sequences that present some of the ludicrously complex aspects of family caregiving.

Whenever I address this control issue for myself or with clients, I always consider what it would be like to have control over everything. Then I would always know what the weather, winds, and tides would be like before taking out my sailboat. I would always know the score before the athletic contest I attended was over. And I would always know, in advance, the final outcomes of the people I counseled. Sounds pretty boring, doesn't it?

As a psychologist I have little control over what my clients do. When I leave an alcohol or substance abuse treatment center with a client whom I've worked with, there's no guarantee that he or she will not use drugs or alcohol tomorrow. Likewise, while your companion worries about the prospect of a panic attack, there's no guarantee that he or she will ever be free of them.

As you know, anything can happen. Overcoming something now doesn't in any way guarantee you won't have to deal with it again.

In any event, you now have some background on agoraphobia and panic, you've seen some case studies, and you've done a little self-analysis. We can now move on to the curative factors: education and practice.

3

Facts You Should Know about Agoraphobia

All of the agoraphobics' caregivers I've worked with have believed emphatically that the most powerful means they had of helping their companions was to educate themselves. In the next two chapters, I'll try to give you a summary of the three major psychological constructs you need to become educated about: panic attacks, panic disorder, and agoraphobia.

Panic attacks are the major ingredients of panic disorder. And agoraphobia can only be understood in the context of panic disorder. Much more detailed information about the diagnostic symptoms of panic attack, panic disorder (with or without agoraphobia), and agoraphobia (without panic disorder) can be found elsewhere, including the books listed in the references. But this chapter should give you and your companion important information about these terms. It'll be substantially easier for you to talk to a therapist or do your own research if you're armed with the language of the disorder.

Your Companion's Panic—and Your Own (Part I)

Panic. All of us have experienced it. It's horrific. Everyone uses the word regularly, and often excessively—especially anticipating bad news. "Anticipatory anxiety" may better describe your experience of panic. That's notably different from what your companion experiences when thinking about panic or experiencing a bona fide panic attack.

Maybe the panic you experience is caused by a more difficult than anticipated school assignment, a new relationship that's going in a different direction than you expected, an important employment examination, poor time management, or being stopped by a highway patrol officer. All these can do more than just knock you off-balance.

You've probably been apprehensive in any number of decisive or momentous life events. Maybe you've used words like "antsy," "jumpy," "nervous," or "tense" to describe yourself. My students sometimes say they're "in a panic" before taking an exam. Some are "antsy" when they receive a grade from an assignment, knowing they didn't put forth the type of effort that they should have.

The panic attacks of your companion are wholly different from these experiences. To them, panic is a meltdown, an Armageddon. The attacks are crippling. And as menacing as an attack can be, the worry about an attack is equally mind-boggling, taking up an enormous amount of emotional and cognitive bandwidth. And that's not the worst part of what distinguishes your companion's panic from your own.

The most apparent difference between their experience and yours is not just the comparative strength and obsessiveness of their panic. Rather, it's that their attacks seem to come out of nowhere. No particular stimulus appears to be related to when and where they will occur. That unpredictability, in combination with the strong physiological changes that take place during the attacks, is what makes them seem so monstrous.

Three Varieties of Panic Attacks

Panic attacks come in three different varieties. There are those that are unexpected, sometimes professionally referred to as *uncued panic attacks*. These are the ones that were just referred to; they're the ones that probably undermine your companion the most. Then there are the panic attacks that are *situationally bound*. These are also referred to as *cued panic attacks*. Finally, we have what are called *situationally predisposed panic attacks*.

The DSM-IV-TR provides clear language about the differences between panic attacks: "Unexpected (uncued) Panic Attacks are defined as those for which the individual does not associate onset with an internal or external situational trigger (i.e., the attack is perceived as occurring spontaneously 'out of the blue'). Situationally Bound (cued) Panic Attacks are defined as those that almost invariably occur immediately upon exposure to, or in anticipation of, the situational cue or trigger (e.g., a person with Social Phobia having a Panic Attack upon entering into or thinking about a public speaking engagement). Situationally Predisposed Panic Attacks are similar to Situationally Bound Panic Attacks but are not invariably associated with a cue and do not necessarily occur immediately after the exposure (e.g., attacks are more likely to occur while driving, but there are times when the individual drives and does not have a Panic Attack or times when the Panic Attack occurs after driving for half an hour)" (430–431).

The panic attacks that lead to and are required for the diagnosis of panic disorder are the unexpected panic attacks. This is true for panic disorder with or without agoraphobia. As a companion, you need to be most concerned with the uncued, unexpected panic attacks.

On top of understanding the different kinds of panic attacks, you must keep in mind another important fact about them. Your companion not only experiences panic attacks, but also worries obsessively about the unexpected panic attack. That's at the root of the diagnosis of panic disorder and agoraphobia.

The Broader Context of Panic

So in developing your own understanding of the type of panic attacks related to your companion's agoraphobic condition, you need to consider the broader context in which the panic attack occurs. Now, this can be complicated. Your companion could have a panic disorder based upon uncued panic attacks, and also experience the other two types of panic attacks (cued and situationally predisposed). Your understanding of agoraphobia must be informed by the way that your companion's panic attacks take place.

Virtually all the agoraphobics I have treated worried interminably that a panic attack could occur at any time or place, unless they were in the company of a caregiving companion or other person deemed to be safe. In the company of friends and lovers, they believed they were far less likely to experience a panic attack. But they still felt that they were looking over their shoulders for the next attack.

A present and available companion made it easier for them to go outside self-imposed boundaries, because their fears were deterred. Still, the possibility of a panic attack continued to have a free rein over their psyche while they were away from home, or beyond some predefined distance from their home. They never felt comfortable wandering through life alone. They never experienced anything remotely like certainty about the future.

Donna spoke regularly of this dilemma. "So when I'm out with my husband, you might not call me agoraphobic; instead you'd say I looked like someone with, in your terms, a generalized anxiety disorder. I can even look like I'm having fun. We can now go the movies together. But, when I'm out alone, by myself, hypervigilant, terrified and without the internal emotional resources to keep me going, then you call me agoraphobic. What's the difference to me, Doctor? I'm still miserable. It doesn't matter whether you think I'm generally anxious or agoraphobic. I just know that when I'm with my husband, I feel kind of normal and when I'm alone I feel like I'm crazy."

In the Beginning

A panic attack begins quickly and gradually builds to a peak. If you've never had a panic attack and you want to feel what the gradual buildup is like, try this. Stand up. Start jogging in place for fifteen seconds. Now increase your pace continually until you're running in place. Keep that up (if you can) for one minute longer. Then sit down. Pay attention to how your body feels. Your heart is racing, and you might be a little light-headed, have a tingling or numbness in your hands, or suffer chills or flushes. Now imagine your body is racing with all these sensations, but you never moved out of your chair. That describes at least part of what a panic attack feels like.

So the panic attack builds, has a peak in seven to ten minutes, and gradually abates. If you're reading along, this probably doesn't sound so frightening; it might sound a little more so if you tried the brief run in place. But the barrage of symptoms and body changes that take place are terrifying and, during the first attack, they're also physiologically unfamiliar. You expect your heart to beat rapidly after a jog, but not while you're just sitting in a chair or standing in line at a bank.

Every agoraphobic I've treated has had a history of panic attacks, although several have not had a clearly diagnosed panic disorder. But all have said that when they had their first panic attack they felt it was life-threatening. All but a few thought they were having a heart attack. What was happening in their body was completely unfamiliar and unprecedented. My client Diane told me that after her first panic attack, she felt that she now knew what it was like to look into the face of death.

Does the First Panic Attack Occur in a Vacuum?

There appears to be a growing body of evidence that the first panic attack, even the uncued one, does not necessarily take place in a vacuum, even though it appears to come out of nowhere. When most people suffer their first panic attacks, they are under some kind of emotional duress. It may take you or a therapist a bit of soul searching to find the source of the distress, but it does seem to be there. As I mentioned previously, it's often due to a life transition.

Life transitions serve as stressors; the beginning or ending of a relationship, the sale or purchase of a home, marriage, and the birth of a child exemplify life transitions that are understood to cause considerable stress (Holmes and Rahe 1967). A difficult situation with a coworker, a corporate takeover, or watching your investment tank or business fail can add stress to a life and make you more susceptibility to a panic attack. High performance expectations can threaten a person's self-esteem and hence serve as a stressor. When a person with some degree of genetic vulnerability experiences such stress, there is the potential for the beginnings of a panic attack scenario.

But genetic predisposition and life stressors are only variables that set the stage for a panic attack. The unexpected or uncued panic attack is the most serious for your companion, because the attack itself doesn't take place in direct response to an eliciting stimulus. Situationally bound (uncued) and situationally predisposed panic attacks do. Since those often have stimuli associated with their occurrence, they're not as frightening. They seem to make sense—or at least they're predictable.

Uncued Panic Attacks and Panic Disorder

The unexpected panic attacks of your companion have several characteristics you need to understand. First, they're severe—harsh and distressing. Furthermore, they appear to be unprovoked. Finally, they're intense, or deeply felt in the body. They can also be frequent. It's almost like after the first attack, you've learned how to have panic attacks.

In fact, it's the increased frequency of the panic attacks, let's say three or four or five in a month, along with increased concern and worry about the attacks, that allows for a diagnosis of panic disorder.

Keep in mind that many people do have a few panic attacks in their lives. But that doesn't mean that they're likely to develop a clearly delineated panic disorder. Panic disorder is substantially less common than panic attacks. Panic disorder will afflict about 2 percent of men and 5 percent of women, according to some researchers (Kessler et al. 1994). The DSM-IV-TR indicates that in community samples, rates as high as 3.5 percent have been reported. Most studies have found rates between 1 and 2 percent, reported without reference to gender.

So what is the difference between individuals who get panic attacks only a few times in their lives and those who develop a true panic disorder? The major difference seems to be in whether or not the person who experiences the panic attack starts to worry or brood about it. A clearly diagnosable panic disorder begins with a constant refrain of worry about whether or not there will be another panic attack, and another, and yet another.

Most people have their first panic attack while in their late teens or early twenties—certainly a time of change. But as I pointed out earlier, there's also evidence of another spike in first panic attacks among people in their thirties. It's apparently rare, according to the DSM-IV-TR, to experience an onset of panic disorder after the age of forty-five.

Caregivers Provide Good Data

The caregivers who have called me to discuss their companions have helped me understand some of their companions' worry and panic. It's instructive for me to hear about the age specific issues that the companions have struggled with, as well as the caregiver's personal experience with panic attacks and panic disorder. If the companion or caregiver is a family member with a genetic link to the agoraphobe, that historical information can be particularly useful. The caregiver's perceptions of the family dynamics are also helpful.

Identifying Your Own Panic Attacks

Before proceeding any further, try to write down the number of times you've experienced, or think you've experienced, a panic attack. I want you to do this exercise without learning more about what a panic attack really is, so please do it before reading on. If you've never had a panic attack and you didn't try the jogging exercise a few pages back, then try that now.

If you have had panic attacks (or what you believe were panic attacks), go a bit further with the exercise. Try to identify any stressors you were experiencing when you deduced that you had a panic attack. If you like, make two columns on a sheet of paper, recording the dates of your attacks and the life events that you were going through. Ed Bourne (2000) has some clever ways of documenting panic attacks. The Web site www.anxietycoach.com also offers a terrific model for creating a "panic diary." The site also provides a fourteen-step explanatory manual for using the diary. (Even if you don't use these, your companion may find them useful.) We'll come back to this exercise later in this chapter.

What Constitutes a Panic Attack?

Seligman and Rosenhan (1998) posit four elements that make up the panic attack: physical, emotional, cognitive, and behavioral.

Physical Elements

Panic attacks begin with an extraordinary array of physical symptoms. For example, in every case I've worked with, the person reported a very rapid heartbeat. That's why the person experiencing his or her first panic attack is convinced that it's a heart attack. Because the heart is pounding so rapidly, breathing is shallow and short, resulting in a degree of hyperventilation. Dan said he felt like his heart was going to jump out of his chest. Other clients have believed that their chest was going to explode. They have described "gasping for breath." A few fear passing out. They describe getting spots in front of their eyes and feeling light-headed, off-balance, or dizzy. I've heard several complain of chest pains, but that has been rare. Still, in the first attack, almost all have thought they were going to die.

The Stress Response

In a panic attack, your body's nervous system goes into a higher level of functioning; it's actually trying to protect you. This higher level of function is a physiological response that's been known over the years as the "fight or flight" response, the "stress response," or the "alarm response." This response gives you the juice to fight to your last breath. The quick physiological changes of the stress response probably evolved over time, and helped our early upright human ancestors determine whether to fight or run away from different combative critters like saber-toothed tigers.

Today, there aren't many free-roaming beasts around to necessitate our hanging onto this ancient alarm reaction, but it remains a part of us. Hallowell (1997) says that panic, "when it is useful, is the nervous system's turbocharged means of escape." He goes on to add that in states of panic, people become "stronger," "more durable," and "faster afoot."

Unfortunately, panic attacks, especially the uncued ones, don't take place at any "right time." They come out of nowhere. Even though they feel life-threatening, they're generally thought to be harmless. Still, those who experience panic attacks often believe they're causing unwarranted wear and tear on their bodies.

Rapid Heartbeat (Tachycardia)

No client has ever told me that they had the experience of "tachycardia" during a panic attack, but all have described their heart going at warp speed, faster than they had experienced before. The heart beats faster in a panic attack to get more blood to the large muscles while decreasing the flow to the skin. The body is getting primed for action.

You may notice this change if you happen to be a runner or jogger. While you run, your heart rate increases; in fact, you can take your pulse to see how you're doing. At the same time, you may find that you're feeling pretty cool, like there is a slight breeze around you even if you're in still air. But you should notice these changes while you're jogging, not while you're standing in a line at the grocery store. Tachycardia in the line at the grocery store is one of the symptoms of a panic attack.

Heavy Breathing

Since the heart is beating so much faster to deliver blood, and the blood is carrying oxygen, breathing becomes more rapid. My clients usually describe their breathing as short, fast, and in their chest. Again, that's what your breathing will often feel like after good aerobic exercise.

Pupil Dilation

Clients describe the feeling that they're in a bubble or a fishbowl during a panic attack. It's like they can't see things very clearly. As you'll recall Dan said he was in a bubble and then later that he was in a fishbowl. This sensation is due to the dilation of the pupils of the eyes, which increases the visual field. If you're going to be chased by wildebeests, it's useful to be able to spot a safe place.

But pupil dilation is a physiological change that no one is used to. It feels a bit like the experience you have when drops are put into your eyes during an eye examination. The increase in vision doesn't help; it just becomes difficult to see clearly. When your pupils are dilated, you can't concentrate especially well, and you may have the urge to run off somewhere else in order to slow things down and see better.

Skin Changes

Many times, my clients have told me that they feel numb during a panic attack. That's because they're experiencing a decrease in blood flow to their outer extremities and, in particular, to their skin. This experience can have an emotionally devastating impact on the sufferer: it's another symptom that makes the panic attack feel like a heart attack (remember that they're already experiencing tachycardia).

As noted previously, the lack of blood in your skin during a panic attack can also make your skin feel cool. Sometimes people report that in the midst of a panic attack, their hands are cold and clammy.

Other Physical Changes

Some clients report that in the midst of a panic attack, their mouth becomes dry and they have a difficult time speaking. Their speech may sound trembling or nervous. This type of body reaction is also common during other disorders, like social phobia. Basically, all the body's fluids are being sent into regions that aid in bodily mobilization. Since you're not going to talk or eat while you're running or fighting, moisture in your mouth is unnecessary. So your saliva becomes thick.

Why Doesn't Everyone Have This Physical Reaction?

Why some people have panic attacks and some don't is a question I'm usually asked in the first session, by either a caregiver or a client. There are a number of answers to this, but the one that's most useful for me and my clients is that people with panic attacks may be catastrophically misreading cues. That is, their brains may be telling them to "run for their life" when they don't need to. They could be misreading cues in the environment or within their own bodies or perhaps even both. More unfortunately, they may have actually practiced this behavior for a long time.

Interestingly, I have found that the panic attack experience can have some upside as well as an obvious downside. Let's look at the upside. Those who have panic attacks seem to have a profound sensitivity to the world around them. They seem to be unusually aware of the "atmosphere" of a situation. In a barroom, they're the ones who seem to know that a fight is going to break out. They seem to be tuned into tensions during difficult negotiations. And they're aware of the various troubles that exist but are not spoken about in a dysfunctional home. Because of their sensitivities, they can feel pain, loneliness, hurt, and confusion more readily than others. Is that useful? Well, it makes a lot of them want to be in helping roles and service occupations. Many also wish to be successful, hardworking, and superresponsible.

However, these folks also seem to want unambivalent love and affection more than others do. And they want to feel that they're not alone. They may be what some have called "highly sensitive persons." They seem to be able to intuitively sniff out controversy and they abhor any difficult wrangling among people. They appear more vigilant, ever ready to escape from uncomfortable circumstances. Elaine Aron's (1997) book, *The Highly Sensitive Person*, describes more characteristics of such people.

As they're particularly sensitive to the feelings and emotions of others, highly sensitive people tend to enter professions where they use these attributes, becoming, for example, counselors, mental health workers, and salespeople. I am struck by the number of my colleagues, people I would identify as highly sensitive, who admit in the safety of my office their different fears and experiences with their own panic attacks.

On the downside, there is evidence that panic disorder may be due to a neurochemical abnormality. Seligman and Rosenhan (1998) summarize data that suggests that the "wiring" in the brain that helps to "short-circuit" panic attacks may be impaired in those who have the attacks. There's additional evidence that the blood flow patterns in the brains of people who are disposed to panic attacks may be different from such patterns in those who are not. There is also research that identifies some degree of genetic predisposition to panic (Zuercher-White 1998; Seligman and Rosenhan 1998).

From this evidence, you could surmise that panic attacks are a disorder of the body. That may be correct. But a preponderance of clinical and behavioral evidence shows that regardless of the specific roots of panic attacks, they can be reduced or eliminated with medication, behavioral therapy, or a combination.

Emotional Elements

The emotional elements of the panic attack are, quite simply, feelings of paralyzing terror. I call these "Oh my God experiences." You might experience this same degree of terror if you were in an actual life-threatening situation. But because during a panic attack you aren't in the middle of an experience like this, the emotional reactions may feel odd, like responding to a hurricane when you don't live in hurricane country and there is no hurricane in sight.

Two other emotional reactions can be present in the panic attack. The first is an experience of being outside your body and numb, a perception called *depersonalization*. The second reaction is called *derealization*, which is a feeling that nothing around you is familiar. Space and time even seem altered. This second emotional experience can be related to some of the physiological changes of a panic attack, such as pupil dilation.

Losing Control

The feeling that you're losing control in a panic attack can sometimes be experienced as being on the verge of fainting, suffocating, choking, or losing balance. These are essentially emotional reactions to the host of physiological changes that are taking place, specifically the increased blood flow in some areas and decreased flow in others. (More detailed explanations of these sensations can be found in Bourne [2000].)

Contrary to how it feels, your body is actually getting into a heightened state of control in order to help you escape danger: there's not going to be any loss of control. People in the middle of a panic attack look anything except out of control. They tend to stop, sit, and gather themselves. No one (except perhaps you, the heroic caregiver) will even be aware that your companion is having a panic attack.

Fear

The most common emotional reaction that I hear clients describe to me is that they're afraid. Fear can also lead to other emotional experiences, like embarrassment. Remember how embarrassed Dan was when he was in the parking lot at work? The fear of "going crazy" was followed by fear of the embarrassment of being labeled "crazy" by his peers. Dan called this complex of fears his "nuttiness."

The fact is that people are not going crazy during the panic attack; it only feels that way. To some extent, the crazy feelings are due to the decreased blood flow, or *vasoconstriction*, discussed earlier. Rapid vasoconstriction can make you feel disoriented and a bit unreal.

Cognitive Elements

The cognitive elements of a panic attack are the thoughts people have during the attack. Usually these thoughts go beyond the emotional reactions just discussed and indicate a desire for some reaction. Examples I've heard include "I've got to get out of here," "I'm going to go crazy unless I can run away," and "Please get me back home or to a safe place."

I've always believed that these thoughts are related to the fact that the body is getting ready to "fight or flee," but that no "fight" is taking place. Running away seems to be the only thing left to do. So these thoughts actually appear to makes sense, given what is going on in the agoraphobic's body. Indeed, in my experience, the thoughts take place after the physical symptoms start.

A panic attack can make you feel like you're dying, which can lead to the thought, "I'm dying, please get a doctor." I've heard clients rail against going to a movie or the store because there won't be anyone in the vicinity who can help if they faint or have a stroke or heart attack. Thoughts like these are created by your companion during the very first panic attack and they are amazingly hard to counteract.

These thoughts also may sound utterly irrational to you; you may feel there's no evidence to support your companion's conclusions about what caused the attack and what might cause another. You too may start to think your companion is nuts, which can seriously work against you as a caregiver.

Any therapist will tell you that contradicting these irrational thoughts can damage your relationship, but you may feel that the thoughts make it difficult for you to help. It's a tough situation.

Behavioral Elements

The behavioral elements of a panic attack are the person's responses to the cognitive elements—thoughts like "I've got to get the hell out of here" or "I've got to sit down before I fall down" or "I've got to put a cold compress on my head."

Basically, the person tries to take action on the fight or flight response. But since there is (generally speaking) nothing to fight about, the typical behavior or action involves flight, or running away from the harmful scene.

As panic attacks lead into panic disorder, your companion can develop an all-consuming obsessive worry about future attacks. He or she may strictly avoid the location where the panic attack took place. Many agoraphobics create new behaviors that let them avoid returning to locations where they've had severe panic attacks.

You've certainly heard of this type of behavior in other contexts. Individuals may not want to revisit the place where a loved one was lost. Victims of a crime don't want to return to the scene. Those who have been in severe car accidents may not want to get into a car again, at least for a while.

The Criteria for Panic Attack

Though a panic attack itself is not a disorder according to the DSM-IV-TR, the manual does describe panic attacks. Following is the DSM-IV-TR's diagnostic criteria for panic attack:

A "discrete period of intense fear or discomfort, in the absence of real danger" (430) in which four (or more) of the following symptoms developed abruptly and reached a peak within ten minutes:

1. Palpitations, pounding heart, or accelerated heart rate

2. Sweating

3. Trembling or shaking

4. Sensations of shortness of breath or smothering

5. Feeling of choking

6. Chest pain or discomfort

7. Nausea or abdominal distress

8. Feeling dizzy, unsteady, light-headed, or faint

9. Derealization (feelings of unreality) or depersonalization (being detached from oneself)

10. Fear of losing control or going crazy

11. Fear of dying

12. Paresthesias (numbness or tingling sensations)

13. Chills or hot flashes

Your Companion's Panic — and Your Own (Part II)

Now that you've had the opportunity to learn more about the nature of panic attacks and you have the diagnostic criteria for them, you can return to the exercise on page 43. And try to determine whether or not you were really having panic attacks.

Perhaps more importantly, if your companion has told you that he or she is experiencing panic attacks, you now know more about the nature of the attack and how it's diagnosed. You can share this information with your companion and urge him or her to contact a mental health professional. The two of you can (and should) continue to read up on panic attacks in resources that go beyond the scope of this book (check the back of the book for some such resources). Panic attacks are a mental health problem that we know a great deal about, and most treatments are readily available. Your guidance and coaching can certainly help your companion get the relief you both crave.

Criteria for Panic Disorder

Now that you understand the nature of panic attacks, we can begin to discuss panic disorder itself. The DSM-IV-TR is quite clear in its definition of panic disorder: "The essential feature of Panic Disorder is the presence of recurrent, unexpected Panic Attacks followed by at least one month of persistent concern about having another Panic Attack, worry about the possible implications or consequences of the Panic Attacks, or a significant behavioral change related to the attacks" (433). Added to this are the criteria that the panic attacks can't be due either to the direct physiological effects of a substance (like too much caffeine or cocaine) or to a general medical condition. It's also important to ensure that the panic attacks can't be explained by another mental disorder, like one of the other anxiety disorders. As you'll learn, panic attacks are a part of other anxiety disorders, such as specific phobias and social phobia.

As I've already mentioned, the DSM-IV-TR defines an unexpected (or uncued) panic attack as one that the sufferer does not associate with any particular trigger. Triggers, both internal and external, may exist, and others may be aware of them, but if the sufferer is unaware of the trigger, the panic attack is still called "unexpected." For instance, a hot, stuffy room that makes your companion uncomfortable may elicit internal triggers to a panic attack. You may be aware of this, but if your companion is not, then it's still an unexpected attack.

My clients who have agoraphobia with a history of panic disorder also have a history of seeking out a number of treatments, many of them explicitly medical (rather than psychotherapeutic) in nature. Since the physiological responses during a panic attack are such that the episode appears to be life-threatening, frequent trips to a physician are not uncommon.

The visits to a physician reflect what the DSM-IV-TR refers to as "characteristic concerns or attributions about the implications or consequences of Panic Attacks" (434). Many agoraphobics, even those who are willing to accept a professional assessment of their agoraphobic condition, often attempt to get treatment for the physical components of their problem. It's also not uncommon for individuals with panic disorder to come up with wild ideas about their own physiological changes.

Ken, for example, had a history of panic disorder with agoraphobia. He was convinced that all of this was due to his "growing a brain tumor." He would make his own diagnosis every time he had even the slightest headache. And since he worried frequently about his panic attacks, he had an uncommon number of headaches. I referred Ken to a neurosurgeon, who found no evidence of any physiological impairment. Subsequently, many of my sessions with him involved his arguing with me over why I was unwilling to refer him to other neurosurgeons who would diagnosis brain tumor.

While the criteria may appear to be fairly straightforward, the diagnosis of panic disorder may not necessarily be all that simple. After Dan had his first panic attack (described earlier), I had to get him to begin to monitor the attacks and to give me a diary of obsessive thoughts he had about the attack. Even though I met him at home and he appeared to behave in a way reminiscent of all agoraphobics, it didn't mean I could immediately diagnose him as agoraphobic, nor could I tell that he definitely had a panic disorder. For that, I needed evidence that his panic attacks were uncued.

People who suffer from panic disorders also have a strong tendency to be regularly anxious, and that too makes the diagnosis somewhat more demanding. So to be sure that your companion is agoraphobic, he or she must monitor the panic attacks and consult with a therapist capable of making the diagnosis.

Panic Disorder with and without Agoraphobia

The DSM-IV-TR recognizes two types of panic disorder. One is called panic disorder without agoraphobia while the other is called panic disorder with agoraphobia. The criteria for panic disorder without agoraphobia are as follows:

There are four criteria for the diagnosis and all four, A, B, C, and D, are necessary.

A. Both (1) and (2) below
(1) recurrent unexpected Panic Attacks
(2) at least one of the attacks has been followed by one month (or more) of one (or more) of the following:
(a) persistent concern about having additional attacks
(b) worry about the implications of the attack or its consequences (e.g., losing control, having a heart attack, "going crazy")
(c) a significant change in behavior related to the attacks

B. Absence of Agoraphobia

C. The Panic Attacks are not due to the direct physiological effects of a substance (e.g., a drug of abuse, a medication) or a general medical condition (e.g., hyperthyroidism).

D. The Panic Attacks are not better accounted for by another mental disorder, such as Social Phobia (e.g., occurring on exposure to feared social situations), Specific Phobia (e.g., on exposure to a specific phobic situation), Obsessive-Compulsive Disorder (e.g., on exposure to dirt in someone with an obsession about contamination), Post-traumatic Stress Disorder (e.g., in response to stimuli associated with a severe stressor), or Separation Anxiety Disorder (e.g., in response to being away from home or close relatives). (440–441)

Panic disorder with agoraphobia is identical to panic disorder without agoraphobia except that "B" in the above description would read "The presence of Agoraphobia."

As a caregiver, you'll want to be sure that your consulting therapist has distinguished your companion's panic disorder (if any) from other mental disorders, especially anxiety disorders that have panic attacks associated with them. Some of the phobias described earlier, like elevator phobia or sight-of-blood phobia, do indeed involve panic attacks. But these panic attacks are of the situationally bound or cued type, and thus they don't fit the criteria for panic disorder.

Agoraphobia

It's time to spell out exactly what is meant by the use of the term "agoraphobia." As I indicated earlier, the DSM-IV-TR recognizes agoraphobia in relation to panic disorder: there is panic disorder with agoraphobia, which was just described, and there is agoraphobia without history of panic disorder. But what is agoraphobia itself?

According to the DSM-IV-TR, the "essential feature of Agoraphobia is anxiety about being in places or situations from which escape might be difficult (or embarrassing) or in which help may not be available in the event of having a Panic Attack or panic-like symptoms" (e.g., fear of having a sudden attack of dizziness or a sudden attack of diarrhea) (432–433). Here are the complete criteria for agoraphobia from the DSM-IV-TR:

There are three criteria for the diagnosis, A, B, and C. All three are necessary.

A. Anxiety about being in places or situations from which escape might be difficult (or embarrassing) or in which help may not be available in the event of having an unexpected or situationally predisposed Panic Attack or panic-like symptoms. Agoraphobic fears typically involve characteristic clusters of situations that include being outside the home alone; being in a crowd or standing in a line; being on a bridge; and traveling in a bus, train, or automobile.

The diagnosis of Specific Phobia is used if avoidance behavior is used in either one or only a few specific situations. The diagnosis of Social Phobia is used if the avoidance behavior is limited to social situations.

B. The situations are avoided (e.g., travel is restricted) or else are endured with marked distress or with anxiety about having a Panic Attack or panic-like symptoms, or require the presence of a companion.

C. The anxiety or phobic avoidance is not better accounted for by another mental disorder, such as Social Phobia (e.g., avoidance limited to social situations because of fear of embarrassment), Specific Phobia (e.g., avoidance limited to a single situation like elevators), Obsessive-Compulsive Disorder (e.g., avoidance of dirt for someone with an obsession about contamination), Post-traumatic Stress Disorder (e.g., avoidance of stimuli associated with a severe stressor), or Separation Anxiety (e.g., avoidance of leaving home or relatives). (433)

Hopefully this information can help to clarify for you what constitutes agoraphobia and what does not. This is not often easy for untrained individuals to determine. I've worked with a variety of different clients who were convinced that they were agoraphobic because they chose not to venture out of the house. Sara Jane was clearly obsessive-compulsive and never experienced uncued panic attacks. She took antianxiety and antidepressant medications to help with her emotional state, but she stayed inside because she felt that she would become contaminated when she spent too much time in public. She left the house only to shop, meet with me, or take a short stroll. However, she was not, in my view, agoraphobic. Mickey had a persistent fear of insects and remained housebound because of her agitation over coming into contact with a large, out-of-control insect. Again, just because she chose to be housebound did not mean she was agoraphobic.

Agoraphobes are terrified by two possibilities: that in a frightening situation, they'll be trapped and no one will help them. In fact, it's true that escape may be difficult and help may not be available. Your discussions with your companion on this topic can be confounding and enlightening all at once. Such conversations can help you know what they need to escape from and help them find ways to maneuver in frightening situations. And if they can begin to conceptualize themselves as experts in their own disorder, they may begin to feel less need for others to come to their aid.

Agoraphobia without History of Panic Disorder

Now I've described panic disorder with agoraphobia, but what about agoraphobia without history of panic disorder? According to the DSM-IV-TR, the fundamental difference between agoraphobia without history of panic disorder and panic disorder with agoraphobia is that, for the former, the central fear is of the materialization of "incapacitating or extremely embarrassing panic-like symptoms or limited-symptom attacks rather than full Panic Attacks" (441). The key word here is fear. If your companion is agoraphobic but has never experienced recurring, unexpected panic attacks, then this is probably the disorder that they're dealing with. It's likely that they retreated to the safety of home before full-blown panic disorder could develop. Here are the diagnostic criteria for agoraphobia without history of panic disorder.

All four of the criteria, A, B, C, and D, are needed for the diagnosis.

A. The presence of Agoraphobia related to fear of developing panic-like symptoms (e.g., dizziness or diarrhea).

B. Criteria have never been met for Panic Disorder.

C. The disturbance is not due to the direct physiological effects of a substance (e.g., a drug of abuse, a medication) or a general medical condition.

D. If an associated general medical condition is present, the fear described in Criterion A is clearly in excess of that usually associated with the condition.

Since I have the unusual distinction of having a substantial number of men as clients, approximately 70 percent of the agoraphobics that I've worked with have been men. It might be interesting for you to know, however, that panic disorder with agoraphobia is diagnosed three times more often in women than men. Furthermore, according to the DSM-IV-TR, the more rare agoraphobia without history of panic disorder is also diagnosed much more frequently among women.

You probably feel swamped by all of the information in this chapter. But it's important that you have some technical data to help in your discussions with your companion and with the professionals who are part of this experience. Perhaps the most important point for you to take from this chapter is that the driving focus of the disorders is the "fear of fear." Though agoraphobia, unlike other phobias exists within the context of panic disorder, there can be an overwhelming fear of a panic attack even without the presence of panic disorder.

Because they're very kinesthetically sensitive people, agoraphobes have an uncanny capacity to "read" their own bodies—though there sometimes is a horrendous misreading of the language and sensations of the body, your companion will remain very much tuned into how his or her body feels. Thus, your agoraphobic companion will probably put a lot of effort into avoiding even the smallest feelings of anxiety.

Many people believe that all agoraphobics have some kind of hermit crab lifestyle, living in a shell away from others. While this is true for many, it's also true that their disorder can go into remission and they can appear to be normally functioning people for extended periods of time. They may not resemble a Disney Mouseketeer, but they can intermingle with others away from their home and hold down a job. They may be under extreme duress in carrying this out, but with guidance, therapy, friendship, and, sometimes, appropriate medication, they can become productive members of society. Your job is to help your companion move toward this goal, and to be available to them when their fears and symptoms are exacerbated.

Coexisting Conditions

In the Introduction to this book, I pointed out that some different types of conditions can coexist with agoraphobia. It's important for you to help your companion keep a record of symptoms or episodes that may point to these other conditions. Such a record will allow you and your companion to further inform his or her consulting therapist.

Other Phobias

Specific phobias commonly coexist with agoraphobia. Specific phobias are clear and present fears of specific events, objects, or situations, the exposure to which elicits an anxiety response. The anxiety response is usually in the form of a panic attack that is either situationally bound (cued) or situationally predisposed—that is, the attack occurs in direct or indirect response to contact with the feared object or event. Fear of heights, the sight of blood, and fear about crossing bridges are common specific phobias. Since your companion's problem is probably better described with terms like panic disorder with agoraphobia or agoraphobia without history of panic disorder, you wouldn't necessarily add on the diagnosis of specific phobia. Still, knowing which stimuli elicit panic attacks or the fear of them can help you and your companion avoid further uncomfortable situations. Your companion's therapist will be interested in this information as well.

Social phobia is another disorder that commonly coexists with agoraphobia. This phobia is marked by an absolute and persistent dread of being placed in a position of scrutiny by others and then becoming the subject of embarrassment or humiliation. As with specific phobias, the response to this type of situation will typically be a panic attack. Again, the diagnosis of panic disorder with agoraphobia or agoraphobia without history of panic disorder may be most appropriate for your companion. Nevertheless, if in recovery your companion can learn to do quite well in all situations except those involving some sort of social performing, social phobia may be part of the problem.

Other Mental Disorders

You will not be surprised to learn that your companion may suffer from time to time with bouts of depression. As many as half of the people who have panic disorder will have at least one episode of clinical depression sometime in their lives, according to the National Institute of Mental Health's *Understanding Panic Disorder*

(1993). While a discussion of depression is beyond the scope of this text, you or your companion should keep a record of times when he or she is sad or feeling blue. If this condition persists and there is also evidence of a poor appetite, overeating, problems with sleeping (too much or too little), inability to concentrate, unusually low energy, poor self-esteem, feelings of hopelessness, or the inability to experience any pleasure, your companion may need additional intervention and should talk to a therapist about it. People who experience panic attacks also have an increased tendency toward some degree of suicidal thoughts. If your companion has panic disorder with depression, you might try to pay more attention to the language he or she is using and the moods he or she is in. If you detect suicidal or self-destructive thoughts or language, talk to your companion's therapist.

You should also be aware of signs of depression in yourself. You're not exempt from these feelings, and your own experience as a caregiver can elicit the feelings of hopelessness that characterize depression.

Drug and Alcohol Consumption

Pay attention to any increased consumption of alcohol or drugs by either your companion or yourself. According to the National Institute of Mental Health (NIMH), approximately 30 percent of people with panic disorder also abuse alcohol. If your companion seriously abuses or is dependent upon alcohol, that problem should be treated first. Signs that alcohol is a problem include a need for increased amounts of alcohol to achieve the same effect, an inability to cut down consumption, and marked increase in use over a period of time. Withdrawal from alcohol can also be marked by anxiety, agitation, insomnia, hand tremors, and hyperactivity. All of these behaviors add to the discomfort of your companion's agoraphobia and panic. Clearly this problem needs to be addressed before treatment for agoraphobia can succeed.

Drug abuse like alcohol abuse occurs among those with panic disorders at a rate that is much higher than among the general population. According to the NIMH, 17 percent of people with panic disorder also abuse drugs. As with alcohol use or abuse, drug problems should be treated prior to any of the treatments for agoraphobia. In my experience in treating mental disorders in people who continue to abuse drugs and alcohol, I just could never be sure what was working and what was not. I think that it is for the most part a waste of energy for your companion to try to address their agoraphobia if they are abusing any substance.

Other Medical Conditions

According to the NIMH, some medical problems can also go hand in hand with panic disorder. Two of these include irritable bowel syndrome and mitral valve prolapse. If your companion has irritable bowel syndrome, he or she has intermittent bouts of gastrointestinal cramping as well as constipation or diarrhea. The symptoms of irritable bowel syndrome can be very aversive, and typically your companion will seek medical assistance if this problem persists.

Mitral valve prolapse is characterized by a defect in the mitral valve, which separates the two chambers on the left side of the heart. If it is defective, it can be pushed momentarily into the wrong chamber of the heart, resulting in symptoms that may feel like a panic attack, such as a rapid heartbeat, chest pains, and difficulty with breathing. According to the NIMH, people with mitral valve prolapse may be at higher risk for having a panic disorder. The logic is that if a person is fearful of internal body changes that feel like a panic attack and has a medical condition that mimics part of a panic attack, that person would be at greater risk for panic disorder. Still, many experts dismiss the relationship between panic disorder and mitral valve prolapse.

Legitimizing Their Concerns

You now have a substantial amount of information on panic attacks, panic disorder, and agoraphobia. You and your companion will benefit from having this and other such information. One thing this knowledge should do for you is to give legitimacy to your companion's concerns. As strange as all of this may seem to you, it's very real to your companion. Try to accept what your companion has to say at face value. Try not to belittle him or her or feel that he or she is foolish for experiencing life this way.

This may be difficult for you at times, and it's going to require patience on your part. As I pointed out earlier, you have probably not had any experience like theirs. Some people are terrified by horror films and others are able to laugh at them. Individual experiences are marked by individual differences. In the case of agoraphobia, the differences may feel disconcerting and frustrating to you. They may severely limit the activities that you and your companion can share together. But for all of the hurt that the disorder is causing you, it's much worse for your companion. Try to stay with that thought, even when you resent how much you have to cater to your companion's needs and when you feel that waiting on him or her is unwarranted.

4

Current Treatments

The testimony of your own experience of panic and the diagnostic detail in the last chapter should help you begin to accept the proposition that your companion's fears are authentic. Know, too, that a description of the symptoms, as horrific as it may sound, doesn't begin to convey the level of wrenching terror your companion faces.

The material in this chapter is not in any way designed to make you a treatment provider for your companion's panic attacks, panic disorder, and agoraphobia. But it can serve as a repository of information on the variety of professional techniques that are available to aid you in accelerating your companion's recovery. This chapter surveys the techniques that practicing therapists believe are the most effective available. The current techniques described in this chapter include behavioral treatments, cognitive treatments, cognitive behavioral treatments, and medication.

This material will assist you in your conversations with a consulting therapist, and should also help you organize your thoughts and questions as you continue to gather new information about agoraphobia. Later on, in chapter 6, you'll get information on different techniques that you as a lay person can use to provide your companion with support and healing. Some of these are variations on the professional techniques described herein.

Professional techniques and strategies available to treat agoraphobia are very numerous. Maybe you know this (especially if you've surfed the Net), and already feel loaded down with information. Still, you and your companion should at least be aware of the standards of care currently in professional practice. If you're asked to assist in finding someone to work with your companion, you should both be able to inquire knowledgeably about available techniques and strategies.

A Word about Medicine

Most professionals will tell you that some treatment strategies can exist either by themselves or in conjunction with different types of medication. Medication should certainly be considered if none of the other techniques suggested in this chapter appear to be working after truly diligent practice. However, in my experience, medication alone doesn't stave off agoraphobia and panic attacks nearly as well as medication used for a while in combination with psychotherapy.

Generally, a psychiatrist will need to prescribe the appropriate medication, although some internists may be willing to help. I'm biased toward using a psychiatrist, because of his or her greater education and experience with treating mental disorders. My Rolodex is replete with the names of doctors who will allow me to provide counseling while they prescribe and monitor medication. You might consider this kind of team-based approach.

Most of the medications used in treating agoraphobia need to be tapered in over a period of time, held at a consistent dosage for an extended period, and then tapered off gradually. Medication can be a great propellant, especially when used to jump-start a reluctant companion's attempts at certain homework exercises like aggressive immersion (I'll discuss this shortly). If medication is the only means by which your companion will practice increasingly demanding exercises, then certainly encourage him or her to get a prescription.

Simply having medication available can be empowering. Dan took Valium for a while (though I advised him not to due to its addictive character). He used it to garner some courage to reimmerse himself in his work world. He dosed only when he needed it, and after a few weeks he discontinued use. But along the way, he tried something ingenious. He understood what I told him about conditioned stimuli and responses (which I'll discuss in this chapter), so he carried a 5 Valium tablet in his pocket. He said that when he felt anxious, he would slide his hand into his pocket and touch the tablet. The Valium provided a tranquilizing anchor; with the touch, he was able to relax.

Practice Is Necessary

Exercises that allow the agoraphobe to practice new behaviors will prove to be the most useful part of the recovery process. Such exercises can narrow the gap between staying home and venturing back to the real world. Indeed, rapid immersing the agoraphobe in the real world without some practice time has never worked very well with my clients. That's frankly like tossing a baby into a swimming pool to teach it to swim.

Behavioral Treatments

Until the 1950s, many of the treatments for mental disorders used "talk" therapies like psychoanalysis, psychodynamic therapy, and client-centered counseling. These enduring approaches were based mostly upon introspection, self-evaluation, and the reporting of disturbing life events. Talk therapy was supposed to pinpoint the underlying causes of mental disorders and help oppressed clients undo negative attitudes and beliefs and become more adept at handling personal problems. Critics of these approaches have said they "add insight to injury." Critics have also suggested that these approaches aren't freely available to the masses but rather are reserved for people who have the extraordinary resources of time and money needed to make them work. Still, all of these techniques or theories have their advocates, though all agree that the work is very time-consuming and expensive.

In the 1950s, a new practice of treating mental disorders emerged under the moniker *behavior therapy* (BT). BT has also been called "behavior modification." Perhaps you've heard some of the innumerable criticisms of BT, as well: that it's controlling and mind-numbing, and that it deals with human beings as objects rather than as persons.

The new focus on the behavioral aspects of mental problems applied new procedures grounded in classical and operant conditioning. These have worked quite well with both laboratory animals and patients in mental hospitals. The behaviorists believed that rather than working with thoughts and feelings to change behavior, they should concentrate on and manipulate the behavior itself. With successful behavior change, the thinking went, negative thoughts and feelings might begin to change into more upbeat perceptions.

These concepts weren't new, and they weren't limited to the laboratory or consulting room. Coaches and managers will tell you that the best way to create feelings of self-efficacy is to perform successfully: enhance performance and higher self-esteem will follow.

The behaviorists thought that maybe this psychology could work with mental disorders. But new strategies and techniques were needed.

Pavlov's Dogs

The oldest behavioral technique is aptly called *classical conditioning*. Its founding is credited to Russian physiologist and Nobel Prize winner Ivan Pavlov. To be sure, he was really an "accidental psychologist," because he "discovered" classical conditioning quite by chance.

While studying the digestive system of dogs, Pavlov noticed that his dogs would salivate every time a dog feeder (probably a beleaguered graduate student) entered the laboratory. The way the dogs responded was so intriguing to Pavlov that he began to study the reaction patterns of dogs and other animals to different stimuli.

You might have heard terms like *unconditioned stimulus* and *unconditioned response*. For Pavlov's dogs, food was the unconditioned stimulus and salivation was the unconditioned response; that is, dogs naturally, without training or "conditioning," salivate in the presence of food. But the feeder became a *conditioned stimulus,* or signal that could elicit a new response similar to the unconditioned response of salivation. Why was this? The dogs learned to associate eating with the feeder, and their glands "learned" to salivate when he entered the lab.

Here's another example of how it works. Say you drive past your favorite restaurant and start to salivate automatically, even though it isn't dinnertime. You don't salivate as much as you might have if you were anticipating eating or were actually eating, but you salivate nevertheless. Your salivation in this circumstance would be a *conditioned response*. The dog's salivation in the presence of a feeder is also a conditioned response. It's elicited by a conditioned stimulus (the feeder) and is, in fact, different in intensity (less saliva) and pattern (lasts less time) than the unconditioned response. This reaction is similar to yours as you drive past the restaurant.

When the feeder moved on to more lofty experiments in the lab with Professor Pavlov and was no longer involved in feeding activity, the dogs eventually stopped salivating in his presence. Pavlov called this elimination of a learned response pattern *extinction.* You'd notice this, too, if your favorite restaurant went through a bad ownership change and you no longer visted there. After a while, you wouldn't salivate when you passed the restaurant either. Like the dog, your conditioned response would be extinguished.

Pavlov's work demonstrated clearly that behavior could be changed by pairing a new stimulus (the student feeder) with an unconditioned stimulus (dog chow). Furthermore, he showed that a conditioned response could be not only acquired but also wiped out, or extinguished. Knowing this, it follows that if you could isolate a conditioned stimulus and remove from it the components that caused the undesirable conditioned response to take place, you could change the response to that stimulus. Now, think of this with agoraphobia. Perhaps removing whatever fearful components you can from the environment can yield a new response.

Conditioned Fear

Over the years, psychologists have learned that they can develop a new response to a previously neutral stimulus. Look at what's called *conditioned fear*. If you pair a loud, penetrating, fear-inducing noise with a previously pleasant stimulus like a warm puppy, you'll get a single, miserably discordant response that resembles fear and upset. If you do this often enough, it's possible to make the warm puppy an aversive stimulus (that is, a stimulus that prompts avoidance). The puppy now elicits a conditioned, emotionally aversive response, resembling the fear and upset felt from the noise alone.

Creepy, Crawly Critters

Have you ever wondered why some people are afraid of snakes and some aren't? If you take the histories of people who are afraid of snakes or other creepy, crawly critters, you find that many had an experience where a yell, a scream, or a parent's aggressive admonishment was paired with the person's getting too close to or touching a crawly critter. That "yell" was carved into a deeply held memory about crawly critters; now the critter was paired with fear of being yelled at. In addition, people with these well-honed fearful memories add a new behavior, hypervigilance, to ensure they'll never again find themselves in contact with creepy, crawly critters. So they vigilantly avoid places where there might be creepy critters. And they're always ready to respond excessively to anything that reignites the fear.

The Color Red

If you were to use classical conditioning as a technique to treat your companion's panic attacks, it would go something like this. Try to imagine that your companion's panic attack is a conditioned response to some particular, even peculiar, stimulus, like the color red. (Remember the Alfred Hitchcock movie *Marnie*? Marnie flipped out every time she encountered a red object, because in her mind the color red was paired to a bloodletting, aversive experience.) The thinking goes that if you can isolate the conditioned stimulus (like the color red) that elicits your companion's panic attack, then change the response to that stimulus, the stimulus won't have the power that it once had.

A Ladybug Cure

Bobbi was terrified of bugs. Like other little girls at the time, she was told by her parents that they were dirty, dangerous creatures. And they felt creepy and crawly and would bite. The one exception was the ladybug. Bobbi felt affection for the ladybug, and saw it as a parent. Why? Whenever a ladybug landed on or near her, she was sure to hold it in her hand and sing a song she learned in summer camp: "Ladybug, ladybug. Fly away home. Your house is on fire and children alone." With that, she would blow the ladybug gently away. She had unwittingly created a new, pleasant, relaxing response to the ladybug by singing the little ditty.

Now, all you should have to do is find the stimulus that makes your companion anxious, and then make that stimulus lose its power or become extinct. Even better, you might try to condition a new response to the stimulus, which, under the rules of classical conditioning, should not really be all that difficult. You can see how easy it was for Bobbi.

This sounds great, so what's the problem? Unfortunately, in working with agoraphobics, I've never ever found a single, easily defined stimulus that elicited panic attacks. Instead, any stimulus described is less well defined. The most specific ones I've found have been things like certain distances from home or internal body changes. Even under hypnosis, no client has ever had an "Aha!" type of experience with me, where they had some magical insight into the actual discrete stimulus or root cause of their mental disorder. But there is hope with techniques based on classical conditioning; we'll come to this in a moment.

B.F. Skinner and Operant Conditioning

The other kind of conditioning that's important for you to know about is called *operant conditioning*, which was formulated by Professor B. F. Skinner at Harvard University. Skinner shifted Pavlov's model around a bit. He thought that rather than just being elicited by environmental stimuli, behavior also operates on, or influences, the environment. He theorized that behavior that operates on the environment has certain consequences, which he called reinforcers.

Behavior, he suggested, was shaped and maintained by how it was reinforced, rather than by how it was elicited.

Skinner would have called Pavlov's conditioned stimulus (the student feeder) a *discriminative stimulus.* A discriminative stimulus actually sets the stage for a particular response (salivation) to be reinforced (with food) shortly after it occurs. In the laboratory when a discriminative stimulus (the feeder) is presented and an appropriate response (salivation) takes place, some new stimulus (tasty chow) is presented to the creature emitting the response. When this happens often enough, the dog's behavior is shaped to the extent that the *reinforced response* (salivation) occurs predictably in the presence of the discriminative stimulus.

Conditioning and Kissing

Some dating behavior is a good model of operant conditioning. Certain behaviors, like kissing, take place on reasonably successful dates. But kissers tend to look for appropriate cues prior to locking lips. When there's a cue—a close nuzzle, a dreamy stare—that cue becomes a discriminative stimulus signaling the high probability that a kiss will be returned with an interested smooch (positive reinforcement) rather than a slap in the face (punishment). After continuous positive reinforcement on this occasion, the close nuzzles and dreamy stares become safe and comfortable cues for a close friend to move toward more passionate kissing.

Operant conditioning can be used in the interest of developing a more positive psychology. Rather than focusing upon what's wrong with people, we can focus upon what's right and work more toward building those strengths through appropriate reinforcement, rather than always looking to repair what's wrong. Skinner would have loved this development. But this approach demands finding the appropriate reinforcers in the environment.

When you work with your companion, you may want to use both tangible and intangible reinforcers to help to shape his or her behavior. A massage, a special treat, or a visit from a friend are examples of tangible reinforcers. Feelings of success at an activity, praise, or your unwillingness to give up are some more intangible reinforcers. You'll also be able to use operant conditioning when you help your companion by modeling behavior.

Role Modeling

A more positive psychology, such as that described above, creates an ideal environment for a common form of learning called *hands on modeling*. Reinforcement theory is great, but you're probably already aware that some types of behavior occur without any clearly defined reinforcers. Some of the things we do, we've learned for reasons other than that they were simply reinforced. Most of us have learned new things by watching someone else try it first. You probably learned how to perform different household chores, drive a car, or care for a child by watching your parents. Then maybe you tried your hand at a few of those activities. Perhaps you were rewarded (or reinforced) with words of praise and encouragement, or even an increase in your allowance. Or maybe success itself just made you feel good.

We all copy. Psychologists call it social modeling. Some time ago, Stanford University professor Al Bandura began to study how learning takes place from a social modeling point of view (Bandura and Walters 1963). Bandura and others have been able to demonstrate that it's possible for people to learn to be unafraid of a particular task or situation by watching how other people behave in similar circumstances. Observing others enjoying an experience that might be aversive to you can have positive consequences.

How Modeling Helps

People can learn to be unafraid of different animals by watching another person handle the animal or by watching a movie about animal handling. In teaching new parents to relinquish their fears about having children, many birthing classes show different types of birthing movies to help people see how it's done. By observing others handling birthing, soon-to-be parents confront their fears about the birthing process, whether they'll be delivering or catching the child.

With this brief background on some of the principles of classical conditioning, operant conditioning, and modeling, we can begin to explore some of the specific remedies that can be useful in your companion's recovery. We'll put these remedies into even greater practice in later chapters.

Applied Classical Conditioning: Systematic desensitization

Systematic desensitization is a process that resembles the procedure for getting rid of an undesirable response (the procedure for extinction). Systematic desensitization originally had a longer name: "systematic desensitization with reciprocal inhibition." It was developed by Joseph

Wolpe (1958), who explored learned behavior and its extinction. But Wolpe attempted more than simple extinction. He added a new concept called *reciprocal inhibition*. He wanted a conditioned stimulus to elicit a response that was the opposite of the original response.

Wolpe was engaging in a new classical conditioning process called *counterconditioning*. Counterconditioning is the learning of new response to a conditioned stimulus. It's called counterconditioning because the new response is quite different from, or counter to, the old conditioned response. Remember that a typical conditioned response (salivating in the presence of the dog feeder) is similar to the unconditioned response (salivating while eating).

Let's look at an example. Suppose snakes make you very nervous, but you don't know why. You've never encountered a snake, been bitten by one, or had your life threatened by one. Still, snakes upset you. As I just explained, at some point snakes got paired in your mind with another stimulus that you had an unconditioned, aversive response to. Let's say the unconditioned stimulus was a scream from your best friend, who was grossed out by anything oozy, slimy, creepy, and crawly, even a worm. Your friend screamed with terror at the sight of a worm, telling you not to touch it. Your emotional reaction to your friend's cries may have been powerful enough for you to have a conditioned fear response to anything creepy, crawly, and slimy.

Now along comes a gentle, sweet garter snake. And you panic and run away. You had a fearful reaction. So why doesn't this reaction ever go away or get extinguished? Well, since you're rarely if ever in the presence of the snakes or any other creepy critters—and you bolt whenever you are—you can never be in a position to extinguish your conditioned response. Remember, to extinguish a reaction, the conditioned stimulus (like the worm) must stop eliciting a conditioned response. For this to happen, you would have to be continuously exposed to the conditioned stimulus and realize that there was nothing to fear—that no one would scream. You would become desensitized and the conditioned response of fear would be extinguished

What Wolpe did, however, was quite clever. Instead of trying to extinguish fear responses by pairing them with the old conditioned stimulus (the worm), he instead created a new response, relaxation, to the old conditioned stimulus. So when the conditioned stimulus was presented, it would elicit a *counterconditioned response* (relaxation) that was the opposite of what was expected (fear). He did this systematically by presenting stimuli that were closer and closer approximations to the conditioned stimulus, within the context of relaxation.

In this case, the person with the fear or panic is taught to relax. (This process will be illustrated in chapter 5.) After the phobic person learns this new response to a level of expertise, the therapist develops a hierarchy of stimuli with the phobic person that are approximations to the conditioned aversive stimulus (the worm).

To illustrate a hierarchy, let's say that you indeed have a snake phobia. Now lo and behold, your partner wants to go camping in the Canadian wilderness on your honeymoon. You need treatment, fast. You're going to try systematic desensitization. Your hierarchy might look like the following (the therapist would provide the snake pictures).

Write the word *snake*. (If that is too much, write the letter *S*.)

Use the word *snake* in a friendly sentence.

Read a short paragraph about a friendly snake.

Look at a picture of a little baby garter snake.

Look at a picture of an adult garter snake.

Look at a picture of a baby snake that you might encounter in the woods.

Look at a picture of an adult snake you might encounter.

Plan to visit this snake at the local zoo.

Imagine three days before going to visit this snake at the zoo.

Imagine the day of seeing this snake at the zoo.

Imagine staring at this live snake at the zoo.

Imagine holding this snake that you're looking at.

Imagine kissing this snake that you're looking at.

By now you should get the picture. Each stimulus in the hierarchy is progressively more aversive to the snake-phobic person. Wolpe would have you learn a relaxation response to each stimulus as it's presented. With the help of the relaxation response, you can remain relaxed through the hierarchy. This will take some time, because with each new stimulus your relaxation needs to be maintained. If it's not, you may need to go back and start over again, or at least move back a few steps.

Most hierarchies are anywhere from twenty to fifty steps. Developing a hierarchy is something you and your companion can work out together. Then you can present the images verbally while your companion maintains a state of deep relaxation.

Different relaxation practices such as progressive relaxation, relaxed visualization of pleasant images, and meditation (all of which will be explored later) can be used in systematic desensitization. Basically, the technique succeeds when there's a suitable, gradual exposure to the aversive stimulus in the presence of an encouraging companion or therapist. The technique is known to be useful in addressing all kinds of different fears and phobias (McGlynn 1994). Learning to relax in the presence of aversive stimuli allows your companion to actually face the fear. And for the most part, the process happens in the safety of your companion's home, so there's no real and direct threat. Instead, you're simply working with material that is perceived as a threat.

Rapid Extinction: Flooding

Flooding (also called *implosive* therapy) is a kind of therapy that consists of continuously imagining exposure to a conditioned aversive stimulus. The technique comes from Stampfl's early work (Stampfl and Levis 1967). I recommend this technique in some cases, although I think that it is probably best performed in a therapy office.

Basically, flooding is a step between systematic desensitization and outright exposure to the frightening stimulus. For your purposes, you can conceptualize it as systematic desensitization without the relaxation but with the hierarchy. In flooding, the therapist and phobic person run through the hierarchy quickly. The therapist presents each step ten times rapidly before moving on to the next step in the hierarchy.

This approach attempts to present the words and images so rapidly that the fear response inevitably becomes extinguished through exhaustion. Since there's no way to escape from the conditioned stimulus, the phobic person eventually is able to coexist with it. The fear is alleviated.

Conditioned fears are so powerful and so difficult to extinguish because most people avoid exposure to the feared stimulus. (In fact, that's a serious issue for your agoraphobic companion.) But with implosive therapy or flooding, the client agrees not to leave the presentation of the hierarchy for a well-defined time period of a few minutes (ten to fifteen or so). The goal is to attain rapid extinction.

If you want to see what this would be like, go back to the snake hierarchy and repeat each of the phrases ten to twenty times before moving to the next phrase. Practicing like this can show you how flooding can be somewhat wearing to implement. I've had clients practice reading each phrase of a hierarchy ten times rapidly to themselves, with their companions present in the room for support. This seems to have had a helpful impact for some.

Narrative flooding is a technique that's like the last step before embarking on real-life exposure. As a variation of the flooding technique, I have clients write out particularly aversive narrative situations and then read them back to me over and over. These stories can involve close approximations to the aversive scene they'll actually reenter. I often encourage my clients to embellish the story, so that some of the worst situations they can imagine (fainting at the mall in the reflection pool, vomiting all over a sales clerk, choking in a restaurant) become a part of the narrative. Phobics can also make a tape recording of their story and play the tape over and over.

Rapid Extinction with Exposure and Immersion

Immersion or *exposure* (or real-life desensitization, as it should probably best be called) is surely among the most powerful and lasting of the techniques employed in the treatment of agoraphobia. With incremental steps, the agoraphobe is slowly placed back into environments that have been avoided.

Prepare your companion for this step by creating a few hierarchies that you can use for systematic desensitization and flooding. Try food shopping trips, going to the mall, getting to a friend's home, and driving necessary distances (especially over bridges where possible). You can also throw in a few threatening hierarchies like feeling alone in a crowded place. In the movie *Finding Forrester*, Forrester suffered a panic attack when he couldn't find his companion in Penn Station in New York City. The scene demonstrates how you as a companion need to be present and available when you attempt real-life experiences.

After working through the hierarchies of the flooding technique, your companion may be prepared for real-life exposure. You and your companion should evaluate when you'll both be ready for this big step, so neither of you comes undone. Your companion will need to practice relaxation techniques and master several visual hierarchies before reentering a feared environment. This will be covered further in chapter 6.

It's important to remember that while immersion is potent, it's not a magic bullet. Your companion must assume that he or she will still be in some form of recovery afterward and will need to continue to pay attention to the variables that can rekindle the panic attacks and agoraphobia.

Modeling Revisited

Modeling can also help eliminate different phobias. The phobic person watches other people have encounters with a phobic stimulus, either on film or live. For example, patients with different fears about surgery, and dental surgery in particular, have been helped to overcome their fears through watching films and modeling their behavior on the films (Melamed and Siegel 1975). Watching films or videos with your companion also gives you a chance to observe other people's behavior together.

One of the modeling methods you can use to help your companion is called *role playing*. When your companion is hard pressed to find a filmed or real life example of a potentially threatening activity, you can role-play the situation, becoming a model for your companion to imitate. You may, for instance, create a scene in a mall, restaurant, bank, or theater. Try to develop a particular scene together. Then you can assume one role while your companion takes on another. Your companion can play-act and at the same time observe what's happening, an experience called *participant observation*.

A useful experiment in role playing involves switching roles. In the middle of a nicely contrived scene, call out a command to change roles. Then you undertake the role of your companion while your companion assumes your old role. This allows your companion to imitate your behavior. Hopefully, he or she will come reasonably close to what you were trying to create. Any behaviors that you'd like to see your companion perform better, you can coach and practice further. Granted, you just want your companion to engage in the behavior, but if you can get him or her to do some practicing through role-play, you can help shape an even stronger behavior pattern. Then you've begun to make progress not only against the agoraphobia but also in developing a better way of handling potentially dicey situations that could elicit a panic attack. You'll help your companion grow stronger and improve his or her self-esteem.

Now that you see how modeling can work, we'll move to a technique that uses a combination of modeling and classical conditioning.

Interoceptive Exposure and Deconditioning

Elke Zuercher-White (1998) has popularized introceptive exposure, a technique of eliminating panic attacks by eliminating the fear of panic sensations. She attributes this technique to the work of David

Barlow and Michelle Craske (1994), although it bears a close similarity to the principles of anxiety management training (AMT) (Suinn and Richardson 1971) and to the combination of classical and operant conditioning that was initially called *two-factor theory* (Miller 1948). She has developed a program that allows an agoraphobic to elicit panic sensations, which may be among the most powerful conditioned stimuli for the agoraphobic.

This technique is based on the observation that fear can be experienced as a response to internal cues like butterflies in the stomach or the beginning of a rapid increase in heart rate. These fear responses are classically conditioned: first comes the butterflies, then comes the fear. But if the response to these cues can be changed from a fear to a more relaxed response, we may be able to extinguish fear as a response to specific internal cues.

It's not terribly difficult to think of anxiety-provoking situations. What's more difficult is to recreate the actual sensations you have with the beginning of an anxiety or panic attack (techniques for doing so are covered in chapter 6). As mentioned earlier, the fear response to the internal symptoms may be among the most significant aspects of agoraphobia. Think of it this way: You may be able to read signs in your body that indicate to you that a common cold is in the offing. When this happens, you take remedial action. Agoraphobes do the same thing with internal cues. If they feel changes come on internally, they believe that they're about to have a panic attack. They too take remedial action: they run back home or to a safe haven.

Introceptive exposure works to condition a new unfearful response to the feared internal sensations of the panic attacks. This technique allows your companion to experience changes in body sensations that might resemble a panic attack. But these changes will be counterconditioned so as to not elicit a fear response. As with other desensitization techniques, your companion will need to confront rather than to avoid the sensations—and with this technique, since the sensations are in your companion's body, they're really impossible to run away from.

This process demands that your companion practice the technique regularly and that you stand by to help and support. After time and practice, your companion should begin to view the body sensations of the panic attacks as harmless. The technique works for agoraphobics both with and without a history of panic disorder. In fact, since the agoraphobic without a history of panic disorder has a profound fear of developing paniclike symptoms, this technique might help arrest those fears.

Zuercher-White recommends that the technique works best if your companion has not been taking any of the medications described later in this chapter. The technique is also not suggested if your companion has a seizure disorder, serious asthma, heart disease, or arrythmia, is susceptible to fainting, is pregnant, or has very low blood pressure. Details on specific practice techniques will be given in chapter 6.

Virtual Reality

This chapter would be incomplete without at least a mention of how behavioral techniques are being used in combination with computer technology to treat different phobias. Computer programs will represent another choice, though at the time that I am writing this, they are not quite ready to be used for agoraphobia treatment. Estimates are that very good programs are two to three years away. Watch for news of them on some of the Web sites mentioned in this book.

Virtual reality (VR) is a computer-generated environment that people can interact with. It often involves certain technologies like goggles and gloves that let the user "move" through the space using head and hand motions. There are currently three types: total immersion VR, desktop VR, and projection VR.

In a treatment involving total immersion VR, an agoraphobe would most likely wear a headset with some goggles, and that headset would be attached to a computer workstation that would allow the person to feel as if he or she were in a space that was feared. The agoraphobe would be able to interact with the environment. So the therapy would be a type of immersion and exposure treatment that, while not quite real, would be more complete than what the person could merely visualize. When it becomes available, however, total immersion VR may require a room or theater equipped with sophisticated and expensive equipment. In desktop VR, the computer screen is used as a kind of "window" opened on a virtual world. This will probably prove to be the least expensive method of VR therapy. In projection VR, a very large screen is used to project a view of a virtual world.

While some evaluative research on the use of VR techniques is available, the research tends to be more of a single-case nature. Nevertheless, some degree of evidence is emerging that VR can be used to treat different types of phobias. Barbara Rothbaum and her colleagues (Rothbaum et al. 1995a; 1995b) published some of the first reports of the efficacy of VR in treating fears, in particular the fear of heights known as acrophobia. Their work involved a virtual experience of views from an elevator in a high-rise building. They found that the work was both enormously effective and efficient, taking just five sessions on average to complete.

Whether this trend will continue in treating agoraphobia is difficult to say. The situations that keep agoraphobics anxious and confined may be so individually different from each other that a few VR programs aren't going to be enough to help everyone. There's also a problem with the realism of the images that are a part of the experience. But it seems this is being remedied as technology improves. Goggles and headsets also remain problematic; some people complain of a nauseous feeling during VR therapy that has been aptly called "cybersickness." And of course there are, at this writing, massive expenses involved in VR therapy.

Still, with all that's against it, VR shows promise. It does seem to be a bridge between flooding and real-life desensitization. You may check for more information in the book *Virtual Reality Therapy* by North, North, and Coble (1996).

Cognitive Treatments

Let's begin our exploration of cognitive treatments with a little Shakespeare. Listen to some words Hamlet said to Rosencrantz in Act II, Scene 2 of *Hamlet:* ". . . there is nothing either good or bad but thinking makes it so." This line is quoted regularly in descriptions of cognitive psychology; it really sums up a central premise of cognitive therapy.

Cognitive therapy focuses upon the manner in which we take in and process information. All of us, all of the time, are bombarded by vast amounts of data. Some of us can drive our car, listen to the radio, watch for poor drivers, and get into a political argument with the person riding next to us all at once. How on earth can we do all of this so easily? We do it by creating cognitive structures, schemas, thoughts, and beliefs. Cognitive structure and schemas are the organizational networks our brains use to sort and file new information.

Beliefs

Now all is well until some of these thoughts or beliefs become distorted or inaccurate. Our expectations about future events start to change. We may make appraisals of our environment or the people in it that are without merit. And we may find reasons for why certain events took place that are far from the truth.

Over the years, our thoughts and beliefs about how the world works become unconscious and automatic. If misguided, there's sure to be a problem. No amount of evidence that those thoughts are faulty will change them.

Aaron Beck (1987) and Martin Seligman (1998) have proposed cognitive causes of depression. Beck thinks that depression is caused in part by negative thoughts about yourself, your everyday experiences, and your future. Seligman believes that depression is caused by a certain set of expectations—that if you expect that bad things will happen to you and you can't really do anything about it, you'll probably end up being depressed because you realize how helpless you are.

So cognitive therapists believe that thoughts deeply influence how you feel about yourself. If your thoughts about yourself are mostly negative, you'll probably begin to believe that you're worthless. Beck shared this model with Albert Ellis, who, starting in the 1950s, developed a type of cognitive therapy originally called *rational emotive therapy* (RET), but now called *rational emotive behavior therapy* (REBT).

Irrational Beliefs and Errors in Logic

Ellis' premise was that people react inappropriately to life events because they have irrational beliefs based upon poor assumptions, misleading data, or a poor interpretation of data. He thought, for example, that people who are terribly anxious make appallingly unrealistic demands of themselves.

Similarly, Beck believes that people's problems are related to errors in logic. Such errors are behind the causes of depression, but they are also undoubtedly related to a host of anxiety disorders and to agoraphobia. Examine Beck's list of errors of logic and think about how they may characterize your companion's thinking—or yours.

Arbitrary Influence

This involves reaching a conclusion without any evidence to support it. For example, your companion may refuse to go to the mall because he or she is sure he or she will pass out, even though this has never happened before.

Selective Abstraction

Selective abstraction involves focusing on one very insignificant detail while ignoring more important data. Dan had given a talk at work that was praised by his boss and other staffers. But all he could focus on was the fact that the company's chief financial officer (CFO) came to the meeting and left early to attend another meeting. Dan felt he had failed because the CFO didn't think Dan's presentation warranted his time.

Overgeneralization

This error involves developing a general conclusion based upon data from one point in time. Regardless of how successful

Dan was at work, he didn't feel he could return to his former position, since he believed everyone would know he was a failure, crippled by psychological problems, because he had the panic attack in the parking lot.

Magnification

Magnification is the tendency to magnify small events into big ones, making a mountain out of a molehill. If an agoraphobe's heart begins to beat quickly, for example, he or she may be convinced it's the beginning of another panic attack, or a heart attack.

Minimization

This involves downplaying or minimizing the very good things that can happen to you. John was never given much credit for taking care of his mother, even though his role was undoubtedly a significant one for his parents. Accordingly, when John developed his own professional practice, he never felt that he was very successful, because he viewed caretaking, even medical caretaking, as trivial. He also had a tendency to magnify any of his personal and professional mistakes, however minor they might be.

Personification

This involves taking on responsibility for the bad things that happen. Meg had her first panic attack soon after she entered the relationship with Dave. Dave thought for a while that in some way he may have been the cause of her disorder; that if Meg were not with him, she wouldn't have had the attack in the first place.

Creating Better Filters

So it's easy to see how the way we attend to, take in, process, and evaluate information can have a strong impact on our beliefs about what's true. One of the basic cognitive skills your companion may need to learn is to create better filters. That is, he or she will need to learn which information is correct to take in and process and which is not. Your companion will probably also need to learn better processing and evaluation skills, in order to confront some of the beliefs that they've created for themselves. A therapist might be a good investment to help with these activities.

Cognitive Restructuring

Change activities like these involve *cognitive restructuring*. Basically, cognitive restructuring is a means by which cognitions and ways of viewing the world are made different from what they were before. The crucial work of cognitive restructuring involves both thoughts and language. Listen to how your companion uses language. Language not only gives insight to beliefs and thoughts, it can also shape them. If your companion's language is always filled with gloom and doom, you'll want to help them to practice new ways of talking about themselves and the world. Again, counseling can help a lot.

Cognitive Behavioral Approaches

Cognitive behavioral approaches combine a behavioral approach with a cognitive approach. Credit for the origination of *cognitive behavior therapy* (CBT) has been given to Meichenbaum (1985). Schacter (1966) also contributed; his two-factor theory of anxiety posits that anxiety consists of two components: heightened physiological arousal and anxiety-provoking thoughts and images.

With a behavioral approach, agoraphobia is seen as resulting from learned behavior. So your companion would work to unlearn the behavior. In most cases, this should be effective to a great degree.

Your companion may also engage in thinking that is more than a little distorted. A change in some of these thinking patterns can result in a change in your companion's language, attitude, and subsequent behavior.

The marriage of the two disciplines in CBT methods means that any number of customized strategies are possible. For example, if you do a full-scale immersion of your companion into a threatening environment (a behavioral approach), you may also want to prepare him or her to use some words and phrases that can be empowering in this event (a cognitive method). Or, if you want your companion to try to develop different words and images for experiencing the world (cognitive), also teaching him or her some potent relaxation techniques (behavioral) will complement that work.

The newest research suggests that when confronted with danger, our senses send signals to two very different parts of the brain. One signal goes to the cognitive part of the brain, the cerebral cortex. That part helps us perceive and interpret what's going on in the environment. The other signal is headed to the amygdala, which is the part of the brain that arms us for escape behavior; the heart pounds and the cardiovascular system is alerted. Given this research, it makes sense for your companion to consider working in a way that involves both cognition and behavior.

Multimodal Therapy

There's another worthwhile approach that's a fitting example of CBT; it's called *multimodal therapy*. Developed by Arnold Lazarus (1997), multimodal therapy is an attempt at integrating the two approaches in a more systematic way. Lazarus' thinking is that people's mental processes, including their mental disorders, are a composite of seven different dimensions, or *modalities*. The mnemonic acronym BASIC IB is used to enumerate the dimensions that should be addressed as a part of any therapeutic intervention.

The dimensions are:

B for behavior

A for affective processes

S for sensations

I for images

C for cognitions

I for interpersonal relationships

B for biological functions

Part of the therapist's work is to try to identify aspects of a disorder with these seven components, and then choose techniques that will work with each component. If there's no issue or problem at one of the levels, you move on to the next.

It's possible to draw up what Lazarus has called a "modality profile," which can be used as an aid to decide what dimensions need to be worked on and what particular techniques or practice strategies are going to work best. The point is to select a technique based on its effectiveness in addressing a particular modality. A sample modality profile for an agoraphobe might look like the following:

Modality	Problem	Practice
Behavior	Staying in the house	Relaxation, outside imagery, immersion
Affective processes	Anxiety	Relaxation training, coaching reassurance
Sensations	Tension	Progressive muscle relaxation
Images	Catastrophic pictures	Visualization training

Cognitions	Negative self-talk	Thought stopping
Interpersonal relationships	Manipulation of caregiver	Social modeling
Biological functions	Weight gain	Exercise

The practices in this sample modality profile are a collection of behavioral techniques (relaxation, exercise, social modeling) and cognitive ones (visualization, thought stopping). The therapist has chosen whatever available techniques might work best for each modality.

A final note: If you happen to do any further reading and exploration about cognitive behavioral approaches, you may find that some of the techniques are called by other names. For example, *stress inoculation training, rational restructuring, and anxiety management training* are all techniques that you may come across in your readings. In fact, I'll talk about several of these in a later chapter.

Medication

Medication is used to counteract the effect of a couple of behavioral processes typical of agoraphobia. First, the environment away from the home has become a conditioned stimulus for your companion, and the response to this stimulus is a panic attack. That's because when your companion had the first panic attack, he or she probably had it away from the house. The farther your companion goes from the house, the greater the probability that the conditioned stimulus will elicit the unconditioned response, a panic attack.

Second, your companion has now created a new response to the conditioned stimulus. That new response is called *avoidance*. To avoid having any experience of a panic attack, your companion has simply avoided any circumstances where he or she will be too far from home. If your companion stays indoors, there will be no panic attack in response to the conditioned stimulus of distance from the home.

Medications can break this cycle by reducing the possibility that panic attacks will happen. If your companion fears having a panic attack, and the medication can prevent the panic attack, then your companion really has nothing to fear and can begin to renavigate his or her life. Furthermore, when the possibility of the panic attack is removed, your companion can see that not only will there be no panic, but that indeed there was nothing to panic about in the first place. Thus, not only will medicine help physiologically, but it can help restructure your companion's belief system.

Things to Consider When Choosing Medication

So what are some medications you might inquire about? Before answering this, I want you to bear the following in mind: First, this information can change with ongoing research. Second, different medications work differently for different people. And third, there's an ongoing debate among experts about whether medications are useful over the long haul.

I'm certainly not opposed to the use of medication. I've found that many of my clients who had unmanageable panic attacks and severe panic disorder with agoraphobia were clearly aided by the use of medication. As I've mentioned, medication may set the stage for your companion to get better by letting him or her more easily develop coping techniques and partake of practice exercises.

There's always the hope that your companion will be able to engage in all of his or her recovery activities without the use of medicine. If your companion has just recently been diagnosed with agoraphobia or panic disorder, my own thought is to hold off on medication for a while as you try the interventions described in the next few chapters. I am also biased toward trying to make healthful dietary and exercise changes first.

I can absolutely guarantee you that no medication offers a magic solution. That's not to say that they shouldn't be tried, but there are a number of issues to be discussed thoroughly with the person prescribing the medication. For example, you and your companion must consider the fact that you're introducing substances to the body that can have some unwanted side effects.

Changes in diet, including an increase or decrease in fat, carbohydrate and protein intake, or the use of alcohol, caffeine, or dietary supplements (like St. John's wort) can have an impact on body chemistry, as can exercise (especially aerobic exercise). You may want to make changes in these areas before deciding on medication. Moreover, even while using prescriptive medication, your companion should pay attention to diet, nutritional supplements, and other medications. Some combinations and interactions can have side effects that will make your companion terribly uncomfortable.

Linda, for example, had been agoraphobic for seven months when I suggested that she consider the use of an antidepressant. She was quite willing to try this because nothing else seemed to work. In any event, she began a short course of treatment with an SSRI (selective serotonin reuptake inhibitor)—one of the family of antidepressants that includes Prozac. This proved to be helpful in reducing the frequency and the intensity of her panic attacks, but she happened to begin to gain weight. The weight gain was particularly upsetting to her and she became angry at me as well as at the psychiatrist I had referred her to. In her case, her weight appeared to be more important than the issue of agoraphobia with panic attacks.

Your Role with Regard to Medications

You and your companion can both talk to your companion's consulting therapist and medical doctor about how to use the different medications. Your companion will need to know some things about each medication: when to use it, whether to use it regularly or as needed, and when and if (and how) to taper off the use. In partnership with the physician who is prescribing the medication, you may also need to get involved in helping your companion determine whether or not to increase dosages when there's an increase in stress. For example, if your companion is planning an outing in a new area, considering volunteer work, or returning to work part-time, these activities may be helped along by the use of medication or an increase in the dosage of existing prescriptions.

If your companion is learning about, practicing, and implementing different relaxation techniques or new exposure techniques, you might want to encourage him or her to consider withdrawing from different medications. Such a change in the use of medication can indicate your companion's confidence in a particular set of exercises. Again, consult with a physician about the proper way to discontinue each medication.

From time to time your companion may not be able to continue practicing his or her activities without medication. It's up to you to encourage your companion to believe it's not a sign of failure if he or she is not able to continue recovering without medicine.

If your companion wishes to use medicine, you can help prepare for the medical consultation. Most psychiatrists have a history of dealing with panic attacks, panic disorder, and agoraphobia. They also have experience with the depression that may come with agoraphobia, as well as experience with other phobias. But since they have so much experience, they may not pay as much time listening to your companion as they should. For this reason, you would do well to help your companion prepare a history of the disorder and make a list of questions and concerns that you have about the medication, such as what side effects might be expected.

A good source for such information abput various medications is the Web site www.psyweb.com.

Some people need to be on medication for a very long period of time—certainly over a year. This means that the initial consultation should not be a one-time thing. The physician should periodically monitor not only behavior and thoughts, but also other body functions that may be adversely influenced by the use of medication. Bodily changes should always to be reported to the prescribing physician.

You may also need to consider the costs of medications your companion needs. Many of these medications are expensive, and your companion may be taking them for a long time. If your companion has no or very limited health and pharmaceutical coverage, try to get information on generic versions of brand-name drugs and explore the Internet for sources of prescriptions by mail. These techniques will help you to cut down some on the cost of medication.

Following are brief descriptions of the major categories of medications. Drugs in different categories are often used in combination with one another, and there are a lot of different choices within each category. This is because people are all different when it comes to both the impact and the side effects of different medications.

Antidepressants

The three major families of antidepressants are the selective serotonin reputake inhibitors (SSRIs), the tricyclics (TCAs), and the monoamine oxidase inhibitors (MAOIs).

Selective Serotonin Reuptake Inhibitors (SSRIs). The SSRIs are probably the most frequently utilized medication for the treatment of panic attacks and panic disorder with and without agoraphobia. They tend to be tolerated reasonably well, though some people find that they lead to a feeling of jitteriness or jumpiness. This may be dosage-related, or the person just may not be able to tolerate the medicine. Some physicians also prescribe a benzodiazepine (BZ) as needed to help to control some of the jumpiness.

If your companion is considering one of the SSRIs, you should know that the treatment will probably last anywhere from six months to two years or more. You can help your companion monitor changes in behavior and side effects (such as headaches, nausea, or sedation) as the dosage level is increased or decreased over time. Be aware that the SSRIs may have the effect of decreasing your companion's sexual appetite. Note, too, that the medications should not be withdrawn rapidly or abruptly.

Here are the trade and generic names for the most common SSRIs, and their normal daily dosages:

Luvox (fluvoxamine)	50–300mg
Prozac (fluoxetine)	20–80mg
Paxil (paroxetine)	20–50mg
Serzone (nefazodone)	100–500mg
Zoloft (sertraline)	50–200mg

Tricyclic Antidepressants (TCAs). TCAs are an older family of antidepressants. They're not as popular as the SSRIs as they seem to have some uncomfortable side effects early in their use, like constipation, sedation, jitteriness, and low energy levels. The TCAs take anywhere from two to six weeks to have the desired impact, and by then many of the side effects will have disappeared. Still, in the early stages these side effects can militate against your companion's continuing the use of a TCA. If your companion takes a TCA, it may be best to begin with a very low dosage like 50 milligrams, and then increase the dose into the therapeutic range.

These are the trade and generic names of the most common TCAs and their normal daily dosages:

Anafranil (clomipramine)	150–250mg
Desyrel (trazodone)	150–400mg
Elavil (amitriptyline)	150–300mg
Norpramine (desipramine)	150–300mg
Pamelor (nortriptyline)	75–125mg
Tofranil (imipramine)	150–300mg

Monoamine Oxidase Inhibitors (MAOIs). The MAOIs are a class of antidepressants that are among the oldest available. While they can be effective, they are often the medication of last choice because they can have serious, even lethal side effects if they're ingested with foods that contain the amino acid tyramine, such as aged cheeses, meats, wines, and some medications. If your companion uses an MAOI, you can work with your companion, physician, and pharmacist to ensure that the household diet is low in tyramine. The upside is that MAOIs can be very effective with panic disorder and other phobias like social phobia.

The trade names, generic names, and normal daily dosages of the most common MAOIs are:

Nardil (phenelzine)   30–90mg

Parnate (tranylcypromine)   20–60mg

Antianxiety Medications

Several classes of medications are used to treat anxiety, including high-potency benzodiazepines, beta blockers, and seizure medications.

High-Potency Benzodiazepines (BZs). The BZs are the most commonly used of the antianxiety medications. You probably know them as minor tranquilizers. The upside of the BZs is that they're fast-acting, often having some kind of a tranquilizing effect in fifteen to thirty minutes, and that they're effective. Also, they can be taken as needed rather than on a dosage schedule that takes time to start working. BZs need to be taken in several (three or four) doses during the day because of their short-acting nature. As with the other medications, treatment is usually begun with lower doses. As noted, BZs can be used in conjunction with SSRI antidepressants.

A few of the BZs, like Ativan, Klonopin, and Xanax, can be effective in treating panic attacks and anticipatory panic attacks—those that occur when a person is thinking about venturing into an uncomfortable situation. (Xanax can also be useful in treating irritable bowl syndrome.) So these particular medications can be very effective in treating both panic disorder with agoraphobia and agoraphobia without history of panic disorder.

One downside of taking BZs on an as-needed basis is a possible rebound effect. This rebound anxiety can actually produce symptoms that are stronger than the ones your companion was having in the first place. Another downside is that your companion could become dependent on or even addicted to BZs. Dependency is related to the length of time your companion takes the medication and to the size of the dosage. Should your companion take the treatment for longer than six months, it's most important that he or she withdraw from the medication slowly, and with medical supervision. Abrupt termination could result in an increase in panic attacks and severe anxiety.

Some people report that they experience an emotional numbing while regularly using BZs. They say that they don't feel as sharp as they would otherwise. Unless your companion can't handle the side effects of antidepressants, it's probably best to start with one of those and use a BZ for quick, added support when necessary. BZs might be appropriate for those times when your companion is trying to move back into an arena that involves large amounts of time out of the home.

Trade names, generic names and single dosages of the BZs are:

Xanax (alprazolam)	.25–2mg
Librium (chlordiazepoxide)	10–50mg
Klonopin (clonazepam)	.50–2mg
Tranxene (clorazepate)	3.75–15mg
Valium (diazepam)	2–10mg
Ativan (lorazepam)	.50–2mg

Beta Blockers. *Beta-adrenergic blocking drugs* are used to treat a variety of medical problems, but are best known for controlling hypertension and performance anxiety. They can also be used to control mitral valve prolapse, which has been known to accompany panic attacks. While some texts recommend the beta blockers, Zuercher-White (1998) states vehemently that Inderal (a commonly prescribed beta blocker) does not help panic disorder: "It is probably not much more effective than a sugar pill" (38). My own experience is that these medications tend not to be as effective as the client thought they were going to be.

Jason was a pianist and a student at San Francisco State who I met when I worked in the campus counseling center. He had to take part in a piano competition in order to get into the instrumental graduate program, but he panicked each time he took the stage at the competition. The medical center recommended that he take Inderal in a single dose of 20 milligrams prior to a performance. After a disappointing competition, he reported that all he really noticed with Inderal was that his heart rate seemed to slow down. He still felt anxious. He also reported that he felt that his hands didn't move the way he wanted them to when he was performing.

The two beta blockers most commonly prescribed for anxiety disorders (with their generic names and single doses) are:

Tenormin (atenolol)	25–100mg
Inderal (propanolol)	10–80mg

Seizure Medications with an Antianxiety Effect. In some cases where BZs and antidepressants are not working, seizure disorder medications have been found to be effective. Sometimes they can be prescribed alone or in combination with an SSRI. The downside to the use of these medicines is that they have been known to have a negative impact on liver functioning. Liver panels need to be done before starting a course of these medications.

The common trade names, generic names, and daily dosages are:

Neurontin (gabapentin)   900–1800mg

Depakote (dival proex)   700–1500mg

Over-the-Counter Dietary Supplements

For any number of reasons, many agoraphobes will not or cannot take medications. It could be cost, side effects, or simply a belief that they are not going to work. I have had some degree of success suggesting that clients try to address their fears, phobias, and anxieties with an over-the-counter herb supplement called St. John's wort. This herb (*Hypericum perforatum*) has been known for centuries for its antidepressant benefits.

There is some anecdotal evidence that it has an impact comparable to that of Prozac. It has also been shown to be effective in the treatment of attention deficit disorder (ADD) in a way that seems to resemble the effects of imipramine. Pressman (1998) says that it "may combine the best of all three of the antidepressant drugs" (MAOIs, TCAs, SSRIs). Still, if you're going to consider using this herb, be sure to check out the newest research on its use.

Typically people take 300 milligrams of hypericum extract three times per day with meals, so the average daily dose is 900 milligrams. Hypericum is also available in liquid form. Like the SSRIs, St. John's wort is slow-acting and may take four to six weeks to have any noticeable effect. The major reported side effect is an upset stomach, but this can be alleviated by taking the herb at mealtime. It should not be taken with any of the SSRIs or MAOIs and it should not be used by pregnant women, nor should it be taken for more than a year. Unlike the SSRIs, it does not need to be tapered off, according to Pressman.

Another over-the-counter herb that may help is Kava Kava (*Piper methysticum*). This is an herb from the South Pacific that was once used in religious ceremonies, and is noted for both its calming effects and its unique capacity to promote sociability. It has been used widely in Europe as a relaxant and has some popularity in the United States as a mild sedative. Kava Kava generally comes in an extract form called kavalactone, about 30 percent potency. A dose of 45 to 70 milligrams is usually taken three times per day. There are typically no side effects to Kava Kava and it's not addictive, although it may have a narcotic effect.

Some other herbs that your companion might consider using include valerian (*Valeriana officinalis*), lobelia (*Lobelia inflata*), and rose hips (*Rosa canina*). Again, be sure to gather as much current research as you can prior to using these herbs.

Diet

Bourne (2000) provides some excellent guidelines for developing a diet that can help reduce stress and anxiety. These include eliminating stimulants like caffeine, nicotine, and some preservatives, like MSG (monosodium glutamate), that your companion may have an "anxious" reaction to. Some people recommend that you don't eat any processed foods.

Highly processed sugars like sucrose and dextrose should be replaced as much as possible by natural sugars that occur in fruits. Fresh fruit might become a staple for snacking, replacing snack foods and candies. Alcohol should be taken moderately, since the body converts alcohol to sugar. Your companion's diet should probably also be low-fat and contain moderate amounts of protein, and should include six to eight glasses of water each day. Diet should be discussed with a doctor or nutritionist who knows your companion's health condition. In the end, your companion may make an enormous change in an agoraphobic lifestyle simply by deciding to eat more natural foods. This will not only improve your companion's state of mind, but can also partially eliminate the weight issues that can arise with certain SSRIs, and improve overall health.

Laughter, the Best Medicine

Often, sick people experience stress related to how they feel. I recently started treating a new agoraphobic client who was able to tell funny stories about her family. She had a routine that seemed as professional as that of a stand-up comic, but she was confined to her house. Though she had never really delivered the "routine" before, in the context of going over her family history, she was hilarious indeed. As we proceeded in our work at her home, she said that she felt extraordinarily more composed after our sessions because she was able to laugh and to watch me laugh at her antics.

We know from the work of Norman Cousins (1979) and new books like *Deep Play* by Ackerman (1999) that laughter and play can have long-term health benefits, preventing disease and prolonging life. They can have the short-term benefit of inducing relaxation and reducing muscle tension.

Unless you've paid attention to the background stories about *Saturday Night Live* you probably aren't familiar with Linda Richman. But she's the inspiration for the familiar, flamboyant "Coffee Talk" character who also happens to be Mike Myer's mother in law. Her most recent claim to fame is her new book, *I'd Rather Laugh: How to Be Happy Even When Life Has Other Plans for You.* For those of you who would like a public persona's real life inspirational story about being an agoraphobe, she can offer oodles of insight. In addition to other personal life demands and losses, she was an in-the-house agoraphobic from 1964 to 1975. During that time she never left her apartment. Accordingly, she missed out on customary parental benchmarks like attending school events such as plays and PTA meetings.

Now Ms. Richman has become a motivational speaker. And she has time to describe how she was able to function as an agoraphobe. She had others do her shopping, and learned how to appropriately disoblige herself from social invitations. She also read voraciously while confined, becoming in her own words, "highly educated." Now she has become her own inspiration believing that she exemplifies how a human being can "sustain anything." She readily concedes that the person she admires most in the world is herself, and she approaches life with a great sense of humor.

So, in being with your companion and in trying to engage in the exercises that are described in this book, remember to laugh together. If the circumstances feel painful, then set aside a specific time to engage in activities that make both of you laugh a lot. Try reading joke books together or watching silly, funny slapstick movies. Laughing together can keep the work that you do together from feeling like drudgery.

In the next chapters, you'll learn to help your companion practice overcoming panic disorder and agoraphobia. Here's where you can play a principal role in your companion's recovery by becoming a coach.

5

Becoming a Coach

So far, you've been given a substantial amount of technical material—your playbook, to use the football term. The first part of this chapter will help you prepare yourself mentally to deliver support to your companion—to embrace your role as tireless motivator. It's a sort of pep talk for coaches. Then we'll get into some of the recovery techniques you can help your companion learn and practice.

Tools for Caregiving

Here are a few tactics that will help you with the caregiving process. They're coaching tools, but they'll also help you deal with your own life problems while promoting a more fulfilling relationship with your companion.

1. Be Optimistic

In the caregiving process, you'll get discouraged from time to time. No wonder: your burden's tremendous. If you find you're always morose, do seek out a consulting therapist or a support group for yourself. But a dependable antidote to discouragement is to steadily expect that your companion can improve and live a full life in recovery. To find this attitude, focus on day-to-day changes.

I realize I've said before that you should keep a journal of your companion's significant life activities, change, and improvement, and of your own caregiving activities. But I'll say it again, because it works! Journaling can help you recognize and acknowledge your efforts and your companion's successes. It also gives you a sense of the history of your caregiving.

Each day, try to find something positive or enlightening in your experiences. If your companion can go to a movie, then acknowledge that as positive, and enjoy the experience as well. If you and your companion set a goal together and it's not completely fulfilled, don't be bowed down. Concentrate on the progress you *did* make toward the goal, and consider that there's always another day. If you view your cup as half full, you'll set an example for your companion. Neither of you needs to wallow in gloom and doom.

Stop comparing your life to the lives of your colleagues and friends. This won't make anything better. If you can't keep yourself from creating a mental balance sheet, then compare your life instead to a caregiver who has to do without the resources available to you. Consider others with severely disabled loved ones who feel, like you, that their lives have been completely taken over by caregiving. Practice telling yourself what you would tell them to keep them optimistic.

2. Stop Your Negative Self-Talk

An important part of your companion's treatment should involve monitoring his or her self-talk, or the self-judging thoughts inside his or her head. Take this advice as well, and monitor your own. (That's not to imply that you shouldn't express yourself: your own anxiety can be heightened if you hang on to your own unexpressed emotions. Express your feelings to people to whom it's safe for you to talk and vent.)

Negative self-talk usually sounds like the voice of someone close to you, perhaps your own critical parent or a faultfinding family member. The messages you use can reflect how you feel about yourself, via the judgments of others. Throughout your caregiving, you'll probably hear messages like "You shouldn't get so involved," "You're doing too much," "Try this," or "Try that." Listen, but only take in what's useful.

Find new expressions for some of your negative thoughts and feelings. For example, if you have an unproductive negative thought like "This is all a failure," change the thought to something like, "What hasn't worked out?" This allows you to start thinking in terms of possible new solutions, rather than wallowing in a perceived failure. (Try a "solutions party" with the family to come up with more ideas. A group can often be more creative than its individual members.)

If you're on the negative, unproductive self-talk treadmill, get yourself off it. Try to avoid self-defeating statements like "I can't," "She can't," "If only . . . ," "I don't believe this," or "I won't survive this." Persistent negative self-talk will cause serious depression. If your negative thoughts have started and you can't get them under control, try "thought stopping." Inside your head, "scream" to yourself, "Stop!" Any time your thoughts start to take on an obsessive pattern, say "Stop!" again. After a while, you'll find that you only need to yell "Stop!" occasionally.

3. Acknowledge Yourself with Concrete Rewards and Celebrations

Celebrating the end of a project or a class acknowledges that you've attained some goal, and goal attainment is incredibly reinforcing. You've heard the adage, "There's no success like success." Well, acknowledging your accomplishments will help you see yourself as a successful caregiver. So take advantage of what's been documented as solid completion.

Your journal is your document of tasks completed and goals met. It's also a record of your caregiving expertise. And while you won't necessarily write a book about caregiving, you can share what you've tried with others in your support network and with other caregivers. Post some of your contributions and personal successes on the Internet. You have lots of sites to choose from.

Regardless of whether you share your expertise, do something positive to reward yourself. It doesn't have to be an expensive indulgence, just something that gives you joy whether it's a hike in the woods, an exercise class in a community center, an open rehearsal of a play, a trip to a museum, a massage, or some new shoes.

If you can't get much time away from home, then choose activities in the home that'll give you and your companion some joy together. You could even develop a dual reward system so that both your accomplishments and those of your companion are met with rewards. Whatever you do, don't deny yourself concrete rewards for goals met. They are a powerful means of keeping your spirits up.

4. Be Predictable and Patient

People with anxiety loathe having surprises in their lives. Indeed, unpleasant surprises, in the form of unexpected panic attacks, are an essential ingredient of your companion's problem. On a less dramatic scale, imagine going to your favorite restaurant and ordering your "special" entree, only to have it taste different each time. You wouldn't be very happy. Unpredictability doesn't make your companion happy either. So be consistent and predictable and remain calm and in touch with your purpose in caregiving.

Patience will also be your ally as you coach your companion in new behavior patterns. For example, if your companion avoids partaking of a new activity, don't express your frustration with anger. Instead, try to contract with him or her to at least try the first step of an activity, then help him or her cope with successive approximations to the behavior your companion eventually wants to practice. (You'll learn more about how in chapter 6.) And anticipate that sometimes you'll be moving two steps forward and a step backward.

Set goals, and times for those goals to be completed, but then let your companion have his or her schedule while you have yours. Your time and your companion's time are two different things, and what both of you need is some room to maneuver. Putting time pressure on yourself or your companion heightens stress and thus increases the likelihood of panic attacks.

Above all, don't push your companion into situations that he or she isn't ready for, such as getting him or her to try to go back and relive a certain experience because you think that immersion in the situation will help. Instead, listen when your companion says it's not time yet. In this way, your patience can be a real gift for your companion.

Ambivalence about Recovery

One phenomenon that may require patience on your part is that your companion could have some degree of ambivalence about getting healthy. People can believe that much more will be expected of them if they are seen as more capable than they really feel. It may help you to know that all of the phobic clients I've worked with found that their phobias were difficult to give up for such reasons.

Jill's fear of insects had defined her world. She judged where to go and not to go depending on the number of insects she could expect to encounter. Although she eventually overcame her insect phobia, she said that she always felt a loss about it. She had structured her life patterns around encountering insects, and ironically, she missed the structure.

Similarly, Bill had a fear of flying that he overcame after twenty years. After his recovery began, he regretted his loss of control over the family vacations. Before, the family needed to drive. Now, they expected him to fly to different destinations. Often he didn't want to go.

Your companion may also be ambivalent about the loss of a pattern of behavior that has become familiar. You're faced with a companion with not just a problem, but a recalcitrant attitude about the problem. This aspect of recovery will take time and understanding from both of you.

Keep Your Promises

Predictability involves keeping whatever promises and commitments you've made to your companion. Nothing will feel more unfair to your companion than your unwillingness to honor particular contracts you've made. This is especially true if the commitment involves an activity that he or she can't handle alone, such as help with a doctor's appointment or the filing of disability papers, or a trip to the store. If you find yourself breaking too many promises, you're making more commitments than you can keep. So make fewer promises and commitments, and try to manage your time a little better.

If you do happen to miss an engagement that you've committed to, don't justify yourself by telling your companion how much you've already done for him or her. Instead, admit that you're over-scheduled and apologize. It'll show that you respect your companion's schedule and that you're taking his or her needs seriously.

A tip: Both you and your companion might want to consider not using the word "but" when you're dealing with each other, as in "I know I let you down, but . . ." "But" is a sign that you're feeling criticized and that you're defending yourself. Listen for it.

5. Be Proud of Your Companion

Tasks that recovering agoraphobes accomplish often involve tremendous risks for them. They risk failure; they also risk recurring panic attacks. They persevere through the fear that a seemingly minor mistake will take them right back to the beginning of their treatment.

Knowing how much risk is involved can help you encourage your companion to look at the potential for change, and to break each goal into smaller and smaller steps. Your companion is courageous. That's not a joke. Carry that thought with you each day. You'll be amazed at how your pride and encouragement can help you both. Clearly, encouragement alone is not going to make this problem go away, but it will make the experience less strenuous for both of you.

6. Continue Your Education

Continuing to learn about new research, new support groups, new treatment methods, and new medications can be empowering for both of you. The Internet can certainly help; start with the Web sites at the back of this book. Government information is always available and current; the NIMH Panic Disorder Education Program has terrific information and can be reached at 800-64-PANIC. The NIMH Web pages can also be useful, as can the Surgeon General's Web site. Addresses for both are at the back of the book. You may also want to attend conferences and workshops devoted to anxiety, panic, and agoraphobia.

7. Learn to Become a Better Listener

You can't become your companion's psychotherapist. However, try to develop listening skills that let your companion know that he or she has been heard and understood. It's never helpful, for example, for you to tell your companion that there's nothing to fear. Just because you realize there's no threat doesn't mean your companion has the same experience.

People with problems garner some relief by talking about them. Listening makes your companion feel valued as a person and as an important part of your life. When you listen, don't take what you hear personally. You may sometimes find it helpful to "reflect back" to your companion what you're hearing, saying, for example, "I can hear that you're sad" or "Your actions tell me you're angry." This technique helps you avoid getting drained by this process, but gives you a sense of satisfaction and connection from your listening. Or just listen. You don't have to respond with anything other than a simple "I understand." When you're listening, don't problem-solve. Resist giving advice, unless it is asked for. It'll probably be pushed back anyway.

Learn to listen, too, to the signals your companion gives when about to experience a panic attack, as well as how he or she looks and feels when completely relaxed. Use the following scale to assess your companion's state of anxiety. Your companion can also use this scale to communicate with you.

0   As relaxed as ever

1   A little uncomfortable

2   Nervous and tense. Speech is more rapid, or the person is completely quiet.

3   Heart is beating more rapidly. Onset of panic feels possible. The person begins internal self-talk about a need to escape.

4   Need to escape is becoming stronger. Greater agitation. Heart is beating very rapidly.

5   Heart is pounding. The person is feeling agitated, light-headed. Possible feelings of being terrified.

When you and your companion both use this scale, you can get a better sense of what he or she is experiencing moment to moment. Among other things, this will allow you to help your companion proceed with or back off from a particular exercise as necessary.

8. Give Up on Helplessness

Some of the frustration, insecurity, and self-doubt that you experience in this process will manifest itself from time to time, in feelings of helplessness. If you're feeling helpless, you probably perceive that no matter what you do as a caregiver, you'll be criticized or the outcome will be less than positive. These feelings are natural when you're in new and unfamiliar territory.

More seriously, your feelings of helplessness as a caregiver can turn into feelings of depression. Early research by Seligman (1974) found that animals (dogs in this case) develop a pattern of helpless behavior when they're given uncontrollable aversive stimuli, like excessive electric shocks. This behavior pattern prevents them from learning new activities that could control the aversive stimulation. In short, the animals give up. This phenomenon has been called *learned helplessness*, since the inability to respond appropriately is learned.

Abramson, Seligman, and Teasdale (1978) added the concept of *attribution* to the theory of learned helplessness. That is, people attribute this sense of failure or helplessness to some cause. These attributions can be global ("Nothing ever goes right for me"), consistent ("I never have a sense of direction or order"), and internal ("I'm a dolt"). Notice they're all examples of negative self-talk. Do these words approximate any of your own internal messages?

Aaron Beck (1987) has a somewhat different model of helplessness in depression. He believes that depressed people have distorted, negative views of themselves, the world, and their future, and that these views are developed in childhood and adolescence. These negative biases can cause these people to misinterpret certain facts in their lives. Some aspects of your companion's disorder can involve a terrible misreading of facts. But you also need to be careful that you don't misread facts.

To confront your own sense of caregiving helplessness, try to remain continuously conscious of the activities you're engaging in or are learning about. Use the seven tactics already discussed to help you regain a sense of control. Realize that even though you may feel overwhelmed, the fact is that you've accomplished a lot. Go back over your journal to reestablish your sense of your own power. Helplessness and hopelessness can be learned under the right circumstances. Don't let yourself fall into this dark hole.

9. Project a Good Attitude

Karen Williams (1993) suggests that among the most helpful characteristics of a caregiver is an ability to project the right attitude. She strongly recommends, as do I, that any caregiver participate actively in the agoraphobic's treatment. That includes meeting with the consulting therapist, attending group meetings, and making suggestions with the rest of the family. Everyone involved ought to be working together, and that demands the right attitude—a readiness to be a trustworthy, committed participant.

One of the arenas where companions can play a significant role is in the behavioral technique called exposure or immersion (see chapter 4 for more about this technique). As the caregiver who assists with this practice, you'll support your companion in taking risks, assist in the setting of goals, and act as a safe presence as the exposure is carried out. In the early stages of this practice, you'll be a major player, but gradually you'll be able to withdraw from some of the process. Throughout, your attitude should be positive and patient— you should nudge but not push your companion. And, as mentioned earlier, you should be available to listen to any fears or resistance your companion has. In treatment for agoraphobia, persistence pays off. And your good attitude and availability to support your companion's persistence are important contributions.

Select Target Behaviors

So now that you have some tools to help you assist your companion, how do you proceed? With your companion, decide what your treatment goals or targets are going to be and when you want to achieve them. Do this together, since you may have your own notions of how you want this to work out (and how fast) but your companion is probably on an entirely different schedule. You don't want to push your companion too hastily or aggressively; however, you also don't want to get mixed in your companion's fear and resistance. Making a list of targets and the times that you both would like to have them completed is a useful first activity. So take some time to list your own desired treatment targets and those of your companion, and then decide how you can compromise.

Once you agree on some treatment targets, it helps to break them up into short- and long-term targets. So you might have one-month targets, three-month targets, six-month targets, and one-year targets. I've found that staying with short-term targets of one to three months seems to work most effectively for my clients. The longer targets just feel discouragingly distant if the initial targets are not met. So I think it's wise for you to proceed for three months at a time and then renegotiate with your companion. Realize that you may have to use a variety of different techniques even for a simple target activity, like going to the bank. This activity might involve a desensitization hierarchy of between twenty to forty scenes, flooding, or role playing. So aim smaller rather than larger. If you have to decide on only one simple target goal, that's fine. Just make sure that you both agree on it.

After choosing a target goal, choose together a treatment or treatments from among those discussed in the previous chapter. The next chapters will supply further guidance, and the assistance of a professional therapist can also help at this juncture.

You might want to develop a table like this one to help with final negotiations:

Your target behavior ideas	Time target for completion
Your companion's target behavior ideas	Time target for completion
Your compromise target behaviors	Time target for completion

Dan and Janet used tables like this to come up with their different targets and timelines. Here is one of them:

Janet's target for Dan: Drive to Dr. Chope's alone	Time: one month
Dan's target behavior: Drive over five miles from home	Time: three months
Compromise target: Drive to Dr. Chope's alone	Time: three months

This method of outlining targets will help each of you experience the kind of optimism that comes from the two of you working together toward a common goal that you're both interested in and committed to.

When Janet worked with Dan on various target goals, she reported that she began to feel much less hostile toward Dan and her family. She felt that they were going forward, even if he was going to return to work immediately. She felt that at least he wouldn't be home forever, plopped on the sofa watching daytime soaps. Dan also felt a measure of hope when he negotiated target goals with Janet. He felt that she was his sister again and that she was a part of the solution.

The list of target behaviors you make can be very simple. In addition to having Dan drive alone to see me, Janet wanted the following: she wanted him to drive his car beyond a twenty-mile limit; run errands like going to any store by himself (in part so she wouldn't have to); drive to unfamiliar places; begin to partake of outdoor activities like tennis and golf with new friends; make a decision about his work; and decide whether or not to go on disability.

Dan initially had substantially less lofty goals. He wanted to drive his car up to five miles away from home during daylight hours and he wanted to be able to buy his lunch at a fast-food restaurant that wasn't more than a mile from home. He thought that he could break up his day by doing a little driving and taking himself out to lunch. He was also willing to try to play tennis with his best friend, Sid, to get some exercise.

Janet objected that Dan wasn't trying hard enough, and was upset that in the beginning either she or other family members would have to go with Dan when he was trying out some of the new activities by himself for the first time. They compromised by agreeing that at the end of one month, Dan would drive his car anywhere at night and up to five miles from home during the day. He would also drive to the fast-food restaurant alone. They also agreed that within three months, Dan would drive himself to see me, drive anywhere in his car, go to fast-food restaurants beyond two miles from the house, and go to the grocery store and the bank. The methods they chose to use included visualization, relaxation, systematic visual desensitization, and real-life desensitization, or immersion. I helped them choose and learn these techniques.

When targets are reached, or even when your companion tries the behaviors necessary to charge forward, reward him or her. Make the rewards meaningful and tangible. It's no different from any other kind of training: success itself feels great, but there's nothing like periodic celebration to make the hard work seem worth it.

So the method outlined so far for helping your companion recover is this:

1. Choose the target behaviors individually and then negotiate the final targets together.

2. Negotiate the timing for reaching the targets.

3. Decide upon a treatment strategy (with or without professional consultation).

4. After three months, evaluate the progress and set new targets, changing the treatment strategy as necessary.

5. Reward yourself and your companion when targets are met.

Using a Target Log

When you've picked the targets and the time lines, create a daily activity log. This will serve as a record of what's been tried, when, and how effective it was. You can start the target log together, but when your companion begins to attack the target activities alone, it's essential for him or her to keep the activity log alone. This will help your companion stay accountable to you as well as to himself or herself.

The daily target log doesn't need to be elaborate—a lined notebook can be used. Your companion should record the date and then something about the day: Was it sunny, rainy, cloudy, snowy? Did any particular events take place during the day that can jog your memory (Giants won the World Series. Car wouldn't start. Last episode of *The Sopranos*.)? Next, your companion should record how anxious he or she was, using the scale from 0 to 5 described earlier. Then he or she should jot down the current target and what techniques or technique he or she used to move toward it. Then your companion should evaluate the effectiveness of each technique—was it very effective, effective, neither effective nor ineffective, ineffective, or very ineffective?

Finally, and this may be the most difficult of all, your companion should jot down any intrusive thoughts that came up during an exercise. It is particularly important to record verbalizations or self-talk about fears regarding either success or failure. If your companion fears failing, he or she might believe that you don't feel he or she tries hard enough. If your companion fears success, he or she might believe that you or the family will expect more than he or she is able to deliver. Your companion may also record self-flagellating remarks, such as that he or she has this disorder for a reason ("It's God's will") or that he or she doesn't deserve a very nice life or good job because "Mom always said I wouldn't amount to anything anyway." Negative self-talk can reflect any number of different issues, especially depression, so you need to be alert to that. Negative self-talk also both reflects and produces poor self-esteem. You want to help bolster your companion's self-esteem during this process.

Thoughts that the recovery process is overwhelming or too demanding should be noted as well. It could very well be that you're proceeding too quickly and that this is eliciting some degree of anxiety. It could also be that the tasks feel too overwhelming and you need to help your companion break some of them into smaller steps. What's difficult for your companion may not be for you, so stay mindful of his or her perspective.

At the end of each week, review the log with your companion. What did you companion try? How effective was it? How did he or she feel on a daily basis while trying? Was there negative self-talk? If so, coach your companion in some of the methods you use to stop your own negative self-talk.

Discontinue any technique that's simply not working. Just because certain techniques and medications are in a book doesn't mean that they're going to work for everyone. You'd be amazed at how differently individuals respond to the same psychotherapeutic technique or medication.

You may want to keep a general picture of the overall treatment activity. While your companion has a log, you might want to create a wall chart to track all the events taking place. Different computer programs can assist you with this, but even a large sheet of butcher paper on a garage wall can do the job.

Both of you should also tell other members of the family what you're doing. This can help ensure their support, and it can keep both of you honest about your efforts. It also says to the family that your companion has a real issue that he or she is trying to work on, and is not simply malingering.

Getting Started

So now you have your list of targets and times, and you've learned some methods of keeping a log and watching out for negative self-talk. Many companions and agoraphobics never get any further. Why? It's pretty straightforward: everyone's afraid, especially you, the caregiving companion. Like any fledgling service provider, you wonder, "Well, now. Here I am. What the hell am I going to do if there is a full-blown panic attack—right in the middle of the first exercise?"

First, remember that you two wouldn't be here if you weren't willing to take some risks together. Second, look for ways to calm and steady yourself. If you feel this much stress and anxiety about the process, you'll find that the relaxation exercises in this chapter will help. It may also help you to write about or visualize for yourself a rewarding experience for you and your companion. By doing this, you'll directly confront and counter the catastrophizing that you're choosing to engage in.

Generally, only the real-life experiences like immersion will come even close to eliciting a panic attack—especially if presented without adequate practice. You'll want to approach these experiences gradually, but don't worry about them yet. You're just starting. You'll build up to them systematically and you'll find that your companion is able to make suitable adjustments. This will be empowering for both of you.

If you still feel frightened about sparking a panic attack, read more literature on panic attacks until you're convinced that your companion's panic attacks, however frightening, are not life-threatening. He or she won't have a heart attack, only rapid heart-beats. If your companion feels faint, it's due to less blood getting into the brain because of the constriction of blood vessels; he or she is not going to pass out or have a stroke. You also need to be assured that your companion is not going to lose his or her mind during a panic attack.

Averting Panic Attacks

Knowledge and preparation can help you avert or moderate your companion's panic attack. For example, it helps to know that retreat from an intense experience can ease the panic. Then you can make that retreat available.

If you happen to be in the middle of an immersion exercise and your companion feels vulnerable and wants to discontinue, don't force the issue, but don't just quit right away. If you're out and about, go calmly to some neutral or safe place where you and your companion can sit and do some relaxation exercises. Talk together about what happened.

These critical points can give you some very useful information. You might find, for example, that the immersion hierarchy needs to be more gradual. Your companion may also find that recording such information helps him or her better understand the disorder at a conscious level.

After the uncomfortable feelings have subsided and you have processed the experience together, don't attempt the activity again that day. Instead, put it off for another time. When an attack has subsided, your companion will feel a bit better, and may want to try again. But try to give credit for what's been done and let it go for another day.

The bottom line is that it is a good idea that neither of you leaves an uncomfortable situation feeling like your companion has failed at some level. Staying, relaxing, and processing in the face of an attack will make any outing feel as if something has been accomplished. Note that it will also be useful to not run immediately to an entirely safe place: running away too quickly tends to build up the fear and potential panic, not reduce it.

When Your Companion Starts to Practice Alone

When your companion begins to engage in practice alone, inquire regularly about how practice is going and whether his or her target goals are being met. Real, genuine praise for the effort is as important as tangible rewards. You may want to include the degree to which different target goals are met in your reports to the family.

If he or she is not willing to try something alone, perhaps you're moving too quickly or the steps are too big. But it may also be that you should continue to make brief visits with your companion to the locations that he or she is trying to work on. It's similar to a new pilot trying to go solo for the first time in an aircraft: the pilot has been through all of the training, but still feels it's too demanding to go it alone. There's no reason to be too concerned about this. It is a very natural reaction for anyone who has a phobic problem. However, do try to maintain the schedule for reaching the target that you negotiated together. Remember that after three months you both should evaluate your progress and possibly set new goals.

A bigger problem would be if your companion tried to handle an exposure alone but panicked in the middle of the activity and returned home hastily. If that happens, practice relaxation together, then return to the scene of the panic with your companion as soon as possible—hopefully within a day. You will have already practiced this activity together, so the learning that took place should be enough to make the activity relatively straightforward this time, even though there's been a panic attack in the interim. It is, however, crucial that you return to the scene together. If you do not, your companion's fear response to this particular scene is reinforced, and becomes much more difficult to extinguish. That's not to say that it can't eventually be done, but it will be much more difficult and inefficient. So try to encourage your companion to return with you as soon as possible.

Practice, Practice, Practice

Once you've begun to get a practice system in place, the work is to stay with a program of practicing until your targets are reached. The evidence is truly overwhelming that if you both put enough effort into the process, the strategic alliance you've developed will pay large dividends. You'll be like any other coach, except that you'll be more personally involved.

Practice sounds simple, but it's not. You'll have good days and bad. Some of the practice will be boring and repetitive, and some will feel like you're pulling teeth. You're going to feel discouraged, just as your companion is going to feel frightened. You will have to engage in your own positive self-talk to make it work.

It is truly amazing what can be done with lifestyle changes. We now know that serious health problems like high blood pressure can usually be alleviated with changes in lifestyle. But the changes must be consistent and regular. The alcohol rehabilitation literature suggests that all activities related to lifestyle changes should be able to be summarized with the acronym SAMS. That is, each should be:

Simple: The activity should be broken into small, doable steps.

Achievable: Your companion should have the physical and emotional capacity to complete the activity.

Measurable: You should be able to see results and to make an account of change over time.

Specific: The behaviors should be clear and not contaminated by other factors. For example, going to the market should not be dependent upon another behavior like driving the car. If that is the case, then driving the car should be the target goal before going to the market.

In all of my experience as a therapist treating phobias, I've found that those who were willing to regularly practice lifestyle changes were the ones who became most successful in the process. Persistence *will* pay off.

Relax Together

Before he or she starts setting targets and practicing them, your companion needs to learn how to relax. Then he or she needs to learn how to use those relaxation techniques at crucial moments. Relaxation is powerful medicine. Many relaxation techniques are available, some of which will be described here. This material will not only make it easier for your companion to cope, but you can use it yourself to address a whole host of your own issues.

Relaxation involves having a passive mindset. Basically, you're allowing your mind to calm down and go into slow motion. When this happens, sensory material comes into but doesn't seem to affect you. Notice how easy it is sometimes to fall asleep in a noisy place, like an airport or parking lot. You slowly drift off and then nothing seems to matter. That is the state you're trying to attain in deep relaxation. In a deep state of relaxation, your body feels like it is light and glowing. You feel like a noodle, because all of your tension has disappeared, and you automatically take breaths that are diaphragmatic and deep. Your heart rate slows down; your blood pressure lowers. Your circulation becomes more efficient, so your body will feel warmer.

Physiologically, relaxation is in many ways almost the total opposite of the experience your companion has right before or during a panic attack. In the panic attack, there are increases in breathing rate, heart rate, and muscle tension, as well as increased amounts of blood to the muscles that are involved in fighting or running away.

There are a number of fine books on relaxation. I like Blonna (2000), who gives a good summary and divides the relaxation strategies into two types: passive relaxation strategies and active relaxation strategies.

Passive Relaxation Strategies

There are a number of quite common and simple methods of passive relaxation. I urge you to practice them regularly and to make sure that your companion becomes proficient in them before embarking on the strategies in the next chapter. The methods discussed here include diaphragmatic breathing, meditation, visualization, Benson's relaxation response, Stroebel's quieting reflex (QR), autohypnosis, and autogenic training.

These relaxation methods are in fact quite powerful even if they appear to be simplistic. As I've suggested the importance of these techniques is not just that they can help reduce stress in your life, but that they can be a lifeline when your companion begins to have a panic attack. Using these, your companion (perhaps with your help at first) can cut off an attack before it has any real power.

In the past, some of my clients have videotaped themselves doing these exercises. If you have access to a video recorder, you might create your own library of tapes of you practicing these techniques and teaching them to your companion.

Diaphragmatic Breathing

I've found that virtually every client I've counseled who had an anxiety disorder also tended to breathe in a shallow manner, high in the chest. These clients also kept their shoulders elevated. What I try to do in the first few sessions with these anxious clients is to help them learn a relaxed form of breathing called *diaphragmatic breathing*. It's like breathing from your stomach. The diaphragm is the muscle in the center of the torso whose action inflates and deflates the lungs. Deep, diaphragmatic breathing improves the efficiency of your lungs because it engages all of your lung capacity rather than the upper one-third that's common in chest breathing.

To learn diaphragmatic breathing for yourself, try this. Slow your breathing down so that you take a breath every nine or ten seconds. Then, place your hand over your stomach and feel your belly expand as you fill your lungs with air. As you try this, inhale while counting from 1 to 5, hold your breath and count from 6 to 10, then exhale and begin again. If you have trouble doing this, sit in a chair and lie back slightly, and your body will breathe in this manner effortlessly. It's how you breathe when you're asleep.

Try this exercise for five minutes each morning and five minutes each evening. Teach it to your companion. Your companion can use it when feeling discomfort anytime, but especially when practicing exercises and coping strategies. He or she shouldn't only use it when he or she feels a panic attack coming on (though that's when it will come in most handy). While some books suggest that you try the technique for two weeks, it's my opinion that your companion will benefit from doing this regularly, every day. It's a pleasant way to begin and end the day.

Add a few variations to this technique as well. For example, you can add some words to the inhalation and the exhalation. On inhaling you can silently say "I am calm" and, on exhaling, "and relaxed"; or you can silently repeat the mantra "it breathes me" over and over with each inhalation and exhalation. You can also try to add a visual picture to the process so that you link up a quiet breath with a visual experience of calm. A number of my clients visualize the air coming into their lungs as a soothing aromatic tranquilizer, a stream of calming, moist, warm steam. Explore to find what works for you and then pass on that technique to your companion. Assist your companion with his or her own variations as well.

Visualization

We all use this technique regularly, especially if we're in a place we want to mentally escape from. Then, it's called daydreaming. We use visual cues to take us away. It's a ubiquitous phenomenon that you and your companion can put to good use.

If you want to practice visualization, try this exercise. See yourself as a young child being comforted by a special adult who feels exceptionally caring toward you. Got it? Now try to recall three more very pleasant memories you have of when you felt happy, safe, and sheltered. There are many images that we all hold that can serve as sources of comfort. These may serve as visualizations for you. You will notice that you may try to hold them steady in your mind, but that they will change by themselves as you fade in and out of relaxation. If you want to get somewhat outside yourself, try to visualize yourself in a peaceful setting like a campfire or floating on an air mattress in a warm lake or tropical sea, or riding quietly in a soaring glider. When you're able to visualize easily, help your companion to develop some scenes or remembrances that he or she can use. Agoraphobics may be hypervigilant and quick to fear the worst, but those traits help make them good at visualization, too.

There are several resources that you might want to check out for added assistance. Pat Fanning's book *Visualization for Change* (1988) can certainly help. Hadley and Staudacher's text *Hypnosis for Change* (1996) also has some useful suggestions and directions for individual guided imagery as well as creative visualization.

Meditation

The practice of meditation originated in India and Tibet thousands of years ago. Meditation became popularized in the United

States with the emergence of the transcendental meditation (TM) movement in the 1960s. TM has a religious and spiritual base and terrific physiological benefits. Keith Wallace's seminal work (1970) documents many of these benefits, which include decreases in heart rate, blood pressure, oxygen consumption, and metabolism, and an increase in the activity of the alpha (restful awakening) brain wave and in hand temperature.

My recommendation to my own clients is that they consider taking a class in TM for the best benefit. Your local YMCA or YWCA may have such a class. It might be useful to consider this type of outing for your companion. It'll be educational and relaxing, but in a strange and unfamiliar place. Your companion, even if suffering from acute panic attacks, may find this to be a good opportunity to practice relaxation.

Meditation may require selecting a word or sound called a *mantra* that you can repeat to yourself silently or in a very quiet voice while relaxing. Your mantra can be a word that's especially important to you or a brief phrase that you find very comforting. Using a sound device like a white noise machine or playing a meditation-specific CD can keep you from becoming distracted. Prior to beginning, you can increase your relaxation with one of the active relaxation techniques that will be discussed momentarily.

To begin the meditation, sit in a comfortable chair with your feet on the floor and your belt loosened. Become aware of your breathing pattern and, as you drift quietly into a deeper state of relaxation, begin to focus less on your breathing while you move your focus to your mantra. Because you'll want to meditate for twenty to thirty minutes and because you may go deep enough to lose your sense of time, it's useful to set a soft-sounding alarm clock to bring you back from the meditative state. After finishing the meditation, jot down any notes that you feel might be helpful in coaching your companion. Meditation expertise requires that extensive practice be incorporated into your companion's life on a daily basis during recovery.

Blonna (2000) points out that you can meditate using different focus points. You can use an object, like a spot on the floor or a candle. You can add specially produced sounds that imitate nature: raindrops, breaking seas, whispering wind, or animal howls. You can focus on your breath, or you can also meditate while walking amidst the splendor of the outdoors.

While it's useful for greatly reducing the degree of stress in your companion's body, meditation may not be as effective in practice situations as the following methods.

Benson's Relaxation Response

Herbert Benson (1975; 1985) offers a type of meditation that places less emphasis on the mantra. His method has four elements, some of which emanate from techniques you've already read about. You need a quiet environment, a "mental device," a passive attitude, and a comfortable position. The key here is the mental device: Benson suggests that you choose one word when you inhale and another when you exhale. In his later work, he notes that a word or phrase with personal significance might be the most effective device of all. You can begin practicing the relaxation response for ten minutes and then gradually increase it to twenty or thirty minutes. When you feel comfortable with the relaxation response, practice with your companion.

Stroebel's Quieting Reflex (QR)

Chuck Stroebel (1978) offers a technique that I believe is among the very best for addressing panic attacks. All of my phobic clients, including the agoraphobes, are taught a version of the quieting reflex, or QR. The beauty of the technique is that it's short, lasting approximately five to six seconds, and it can be elicited almost like a classically conditioned response to a stressor. It utilizes diaphragmatic breathing, muscle relaxation, and visualizations. I have developed a slightly modified version of the technique, which I learned from my colleague Erik Peper. Here it is:

1. Smile a big, goofy smile.

2. Sparkle your eyes by simultaneously blinking them rapidly and shifting them from left to right.

3. Take a three-second, deep, diaphragmatic breath and exhale.

4. Drop your shoulders.

5. Imagine your right arm and left arm warming as you visualize moderately hot air coming down each arm.

This technique can be learned best by practicing it each morning and evening. I recommend that my new phobic clients practice the technique at least fifty times in the morning and in the evening. It only takes a few seconds to complete each repetition, and the increased practice helps make it close to an unconscious response in the face of a specific stressor. It can be used in the presence of all phobic stressors, but is particularly useful in crowds or social situations. When you coach your companion in this technique, get him or her to start with a really stupid, silly grin. The laughter that ensues makes the QR even more effective for quick relaxation.

Autohypnosis and Autogenic Training

I'll mention two last methods of relaxation only briefly, and recommend some reading and exercises that you can do together with your companion to learn them.

Autohypnosis. Hypnosis is a highly relaxed state of consciousness. A hypnotized person is both at peace and highly receptive to suggestion from others. The latter is the crucial component of the technique for your agoraphobic companion. Either you or your companion can make hypnotic suggestions that will enhance his or her life.

Having already developed a degree of skill with some of the relaxation techniques, you should both be able to learn autohypnosis, or self-hypnosis. A good book to teach it to you is Hadley and Staudacher's *Hypnosis for Change* (1996). Another excellent book for you and your companion to share is *Hypnosis with Friends and Lovers* by Freda Morris (1979). These guides offer step-by-step approaches and they're easy to understand. You can practice the strategies by serving as a coach to your companion. But let your companion try the techniques on you as well.

As a quick introduction to the practice, here is my ninety-second autohypnotic method:

1. Take off your shoes, loosen your belt, remove your contact lenses, and sit down in an armchair with your legs uncrossed and your arms on the chair's arms. Now relax.

2. Roll your eyes way up to the top of your head and hold them there for ten seconds. Then bring them down to center and slowly close them.

3. Squeeze your hands into tight fists and imagine that you've glued them to a very sticky ball. You can't open your fingers and palms. The more you try, the faster the glue dries.

4. Now, take yourself deeper into this state by counting backwards from 10 to 1. After each number, say, "I'm going even deeper." Continue to let the glue harden.

5. As your hands remain tightly closed, your body has become completely relaxed and very heavy, and your mind has become more open to suggestion.

6. Give yourself a pleasant suggestion that is related to a desired outcome. Try something like these: "My patience is eternal"; "My outlook is positive"; "I love to coach."

7. Now that you have finished the suggestion, count up from 1 to 10. After each number, say, "I'm coming up." The glue will begin to soften, turning to water. At 10, say, "I'm completely balanced."

8. Now slowly open your hands. As you do so you will begin to become completely refreshed and awake.

9. Now slowly open your eyes. You've just experienced ninety seconds worth of autohypnosis.

Autogenic Training. *Autogenic training* is a technique that's similar to hypnosis. Developed by Johannes Schultz and Wolfgang Luthe (1959), it uses specific visual images of your body to help you become warm and relaxed. Blonna (2000) affirms that autogenics relaxes your body and then your mind, whereas a technique like meditation relaxes your body after relaxing your mind. Autogenics focuses upon the following methods, which you can teach to your companion. You can also try this technique for yourself. My modifications were developed with Erik Peper. First read through the steps until you can remember them without looking at them. You may want to make a tape of you own voice reading through the steps to help you practice.

1. Sit comfortably or lie down, and close your eyes.

2. Take several diaphragmatic breaths. Focus upon and relax any tense muscles. Then repeat sentences to yourself like "My breathing is slow and steady, " "My breathing is smooth and rhythmic," or "My breathing is effortless and calm." You can create visual images of you lying on an air mattress in very warm tropical waters, allowing the waters to sweep gently over you, warming your chest and shoulders and thighs.

3. Continue to breathe slowly, diaphragmatically, and regularly. When you're aware of your body warming, visualize the soft, gentle pumping of your heart and then say, "My heartbeat is calm and even." Develop your visualization so that you can see your blood flowing gently, smoothly, and efficiently throughout your body, from your nose to your toes, meandering its way through the precious organs of your being. Then, when you're ready, visualize the center of your body, your solar plexus, and allow the efficiency of your circulation to permit you to say, "My solar plexus is warm and relaxed." Then repeat these words or similar ones. "I'm relaxed"; "I'm calm"; "I'm quiet"; "My breathing is smooth, effortless, and

rhythmic"; "My heartbeat is calm and even"; "My solar plexus is warm and relaxed." When you're ready, move on to the next step.

4. Focus your attention on each arm, visualizing the warmth of the rich, deep-red blood traversing the arteries and veins on its long journey. Begin with your right arm and hand. Say, "My right arm and hand are heavy and warm." Do the same visualization with the left arm and hand and repeat the phrase, "My left arm and hand are heavy and warm." Now try the same visualization with both your arms and hands at once and repeat, "Both of my arms are heavy and warm. It would take a huge effort to raise my arms. They are very, very heavy." Continue your relaxed diaphragmatic breathing and imagine the gentle flow of the warming blood through your limbs making them feel very, very warm.

5. Now, with your body heavy and warm, allow your breathing to remain slow, steady, and deep. When you're ready, attend to your right leg and foot and repeat, "My right leg and foot are heavy and warm." Now shift your attention to your left leg and foot and repeat, "My left leg and foot are heavy and warm." Now turn your attention to both of your legs and repeat, "Both of my legs are heavy and warm. It would take quite an effort to lift up my legs and feet. They are very, very heavy."

6. As you finish now with your limbs, imagine the calm and the warmth covering you so that you are both deeply relaxed and comfortable. As you breathe deeply, repeat, "I'm calm and relaxed." Repeat the phrase again and again, in rhythm with your breath: "I'm calm and relaxed." When you're feeling completely relaxed and done with the exercise, begin a backwards countdown from five to one. Say the number to yourself and then carry out the recommended behavior:

5. Take a deep, diaphragmatic breath, and picture the room you're in.

4. Take another diaphragmatic breath and begin a slow stretch of your spine, legs, and arms.

3. As you take another diaphragmatic breath, slowly open your eyes.

2. Take a final deep breath and allow yourself to become more and more mentally alert.

1. Keep breathing as you let yourself become completely alert and fully awake, and when you're ready, get up from the position you're in.

This technique is a good one for you and your companion to practice together, coaching each other.

Active Relaxation Strategies

Active relaxation strategies differ from the passive strategies in that they use physical techniques, reducing muscle tension while calming the body. In this part of the chapter, which partially uses Blonna's (2000) suggestions, we'll cover Jacobsonian progressive muscle relaxation (PMR), yoga, massage, therapeutic touch, and aerobic exercise.

Jacobsonian Progressive Muscle Relaxation

Before beginning this section, I'd like you to feel how stress and tension can be held in your body without your being aware of it. For a moment, make a fist with your right hand and hold it tightly. After about ten seconds, hold it even more tightly, and keep this pose for thirty seconds. You'll notice that after about twenty seconds, you don't feel pain; in fact your hand has become numb and just seems to float. After you've achieved the state of numbness, slowly open your hand. Notice how your hand hurts as you open it and how stiff all of your muscles and joints are. This shows how tension can do so much harm to your body while you're unaware of what's happening to you.

Edmund Jacobson (1970), being aware of how nervous and tense his surgical patients were, developed a method called progressive muscle relaxation (PMR) to help them relax before surgical intervention. He believed it would aid in their post-operative recovery. He made them aware of the tension in their bodies and then taught them how to release the tension. While teaching his relaxation technique, he saw that by learning to relax the muscles, patients could also learn to relax the mind. He further realized that the technique could prevent muscle tension from building up, thus making it not only a therapeutic approach but also a preventative one. It has since had a positive impact on a range of problems, from hypertension to ulcerative colitis. Further research has found that PMR helps improve concentration while decreasing anxiety, both significant indicators of a successful recovery from agoraphobia.

Basically, PMR uses the method of tensing or contracting the muscles of the body and then relaxing them. You start at the toes and work your way up to your face and forehead. Should you and your companion choose to use this technique, you'll want to set aside twenty minutes or so for the whole exercise, preferably twice a day. Your companion may want to do it more frequently, especially before taking part in some form of recovery exercise. Try to schedule PMR at approximately the same time each day. For this as well as all of the other relaxation techniques, practice in a place that is quiet and free from any distractions. Before beginning, be sure that your clothing is loose and your belt is unfastened. You may also want to incorporate words, phrases, or mantras from the passive relaxation techniques.

Lie on your back with your arms at your sides and your legs bent slightly. Now try the following abbreviated version of PMR, which I use with my clients.

1. Point your toes away from your face and hold them in that position for a count of five. (We'll always hold a pose for a count of five.) Release, and relax for a count of five. (After a count of five, we'll tense another group of muscles and continue this procedure until the exercise is over. We'll always relax for a five-count between muscle contractions.)

2. Point your toes to the sky and stretch your ankles.

3. Squeeze your calves by slightly raising your knees.

4. Contract your thighs.

5. Tense your stomach by pulling your upper torso off the ground about three inches.

6. Tighten the muscles in your buttocks and anus.

7. Arch your back, putting pressure on your shoulders and buttocks.

8. Lift your shoulders up beyond your ears.

9. Make fists and clench your lower arms.

10. Clench your fists and tense your upper arms.

11. Lift up your head and place your chin on your breast.

12. Lean your head back, so your neck is stretched out.

13. Turn your head to the right, stretching it as far as you can.

14. Turn your head to the left, stretching it as far as you can.

15. Tighten your face into a goofy, puckered expression.

16. Stretch your eyes wide open so that your forehead wrinkles.

If you like, repeat the exercise. Some of my clients like to take the exercise up to their heads and then back down to their toes. I call this going from your toes to your nose to your toes. You and your companion may wish to coach each other in this exercise.

Yoga, Yoga Stretch, and Mat Work

If you have a dog or a cat and you watch it get up from a nap, you'll notice that it engages in very sophisticated, smooth stretches. It curls its spine, or it places one leg and then the other in front or behind itself and, again, raises and lowers its spine. It seems to do this after every period of relaxed sleep. Unfortunately, few of us stretch naturally like dogs and cats. However, by using yoga or yoga stretches, we can imitate dogs and cats and reduce both muscle tension and the stressful communications that these tense muscles send to our brains.

Yoga instruction involves the integration of spiritual, mental, physical, and social ways of being. Its focus is on carrying yourself in a relaxed way, maintaining a good posture with which to address the world. While yoga has many other aspects, it's really the asanas, or physical postures, that help you most to stretch your body.

Yoga that's involved with the stretching of the body is called *hatha yoga*. One of the benefits of this method of yoga is the achievement of a high level of flexibility. While more information on the technique is beyond the scope of this book, many different types of classes are available that you and your companion can participate in. Schools, places of spiritual worship, health clubs, and the YMCA or YWCA are all facilities that may offer yoga classes. Such classes may be called yoga, yoga stretch, hatha yoga, or even "mat work." In the class, you'll learn to imitate animals with stretches like downward dog, upward cat, and lion and stork poses. You'll stretch out further with toe and sky touches, side bends, shoulder rolls, and back stretches. Yoga is fine practice to prepare for different therapeutic techniques like real life desensitization (immersion).

Massage

If you and your companion want to share an interesting treat together, try having a massage. A massage will both help you relax and stimulate your tissues and muscles. This will increase your blood circulation and make you feel warm and comfortable. There are a variety of different forms of massage, including shiatsu, Swedish, sensual, amma, and athletic.

Shiatsu massage is a form of fingertip massage that manipulates pressure points in the body called chakras. It also utilizes deep relaxation to remove energy blocks that hinder the body's functions. Shiatsu improves circulation and stimulates the nervous system. It's usually done while you're dressed. Swedish massage is the most common form of massage and is usually done when you're naked.

It's a total body massage, using a range of pressure from light strokes to heavier ones. Sensual massage provides erotic pleasure and satisfaction to another person in an intimate experience. Amma massage is designed to stimulate the nerves that are believed to produce organic disorders, on the theory that stimulating these nerves treats the illness. Athletic massage typically focuses upon a sports-related injury or upon muscle fatigue. The massage concentrates on the injured or fatigued area.

There are any number of interesting how-to books on sensual or therapeutic massage. A whole literature on athletic massage can usually be found in the sports section at a bookstore. It's my own belief that before trying to give a massage to your companion or having your companion give one to you, you get several professional massages so that you know what a good one feels like and you have an understanding of how different degrees and types of pressure feel. The American Massage Therapy Association can direct you to a massage therapist in your area. Their Web site address is at the back of the book.

Therapeutic Touch

This approach is probably among the least scientifically tested approaches to active relaxation but, like yoga, it's also one of the oldest: the Bible refers to the "laying on of hands." Since becoming more recently popularized by Krieger's book on bodywork (1979), it's now more often referred to as *therapeutic touch.*

Touch has long been used as a way to enhance the effectiveness of communication. Waiters and waitresses often report that they receive larger tips when they touch the shoulder of a diner when presenting the check. Hellos and goodbyes are frequently accompanied by some kind of touching, like a kiss, a hug, or a handshake.

The power of therapeutic touch is in what Krieger believes is an "energy transfer" between people. The idea is that positive energy can be transferred between two people—for examples, between you and your companion. Look at how good a simple hug can feel. Note how children like to nuzzle up to their parents for body contact.

While therapeutic touch is not a common method of relaxation, knowing about it can sensitize you to the fact that the simple act of touching can have healing powers. A lonely person like a shut-in or an agoraphobic could be helped significantly with a mere touch.

I've suggested to my clients' companions that they try the following: Rub your hands together rapidly so that they become very warm. Then shake them out, and place them on the forehead of your partner. Or, after warming your hands through rubbing, place one hand on the back of your companion's neck and the other on his or her shoulders as the two of you stand together. You can add a few words that suggest relaxation, and your companion will slowly drift into a nicely altered state of relaxation.

Aerobic Exercise

Now, your companion may have refused to try any of the relaxation techniques mentioned so far. But there's a final one to try: aerobic exercise—and not just if all else fails, but because it contributes so much to well-being. It's not healthy or beneficial for your companion to hang around the house without trying to get a little more fit. Being a couch potato just builds up energy. If your companion is under stress, aerobic exercise can release it.

Aerobic exercise consists of any activity that consumes oxygen. Such activities include sustained (lasting more than five minutes) biking, running, jogging, rowing, or swimming. Aerobic activity allows for the production of adenosine triphosphate (ATP), a compound that's an energy resource in the body. This production is sometimes called the "afterburn" of aerobic exercise: even after you stop, your body is still smoldering off calories at an increased rate.

Sustained aerobic exercise can yield a pleasant euphoria resulting from the release of endorphins, brain chemicals that seem to not only block pain and discomfort but also produce a kind of "high" (sometimes called a "runner's high"). Furthermore, exercise helps to release the neurotransmitters serotonin, dopamine, and norepinephrine. These brain chemicals can add to the "high" produced by the endorphins because they diminish depression and increase a sense of well-being. Remember how often serotonin reuptake inhibitors (SSRIs) are a part of the panic attack drug treatment? Aerobic exercise could have the same effect while being substantially cheaper. After exercise, the body is also more relaxed because it's tired.

So, exercise can enhance good moods, help keep your companion fit, and add to a better sense of well-being. Sounds like you could benefit from it, too! With the resulting positive outlook, you'll be ready to take on some of the more demanding techniques of being a caregiver and a partner in your companion's recovery.

6

Practice Exercises and Coping Strategies

So now it's high time to let the rubber hit the road. Drawing upon what's already been discussed, this chapter will give you some specific step-by-step practice strategies to coach your companion through the recovery process. This material is prescribed in the same order as the techniques discussed in chapter 4, starting with behavioral techniques, then moving to cognitive work, and ending with some cognitive behavioral approaches.

Systematic Desensitization

Before you begin a program of systematic desensitization, work with your companion to develop topflight competency in the relaxation techniques in chapter 5. This is of utmost importance. The desensitization therapy that I'll describe here requires that your companion be able to relax very, very quickly, almost on command. If your companion hasn't yet mastered this ability, back up and work on it together. The quieting reflex (QR) should be particularly helpful; it's among the easiest and quickest of the relaxation techniques to become proficient in.

In this process you're going to verbally present frightening stimuli to your companion in a hierarchy from least feared stimulus to most feared. The idea is to sap the power of the feared stimulus, or make it extinct.

We'll also use Wolpe's concept of reciprocal inhibition (1958). That is, we'll condition a new positive response to the scary stimulus; the new response will actually block the feared response. In this case we'll use a relaxation response. If it can become stronger than the feared response, then your companion will be on the road to recovery.

The two keys to the process are that the exposure to increasingly fear-provoking stimuli is incremental and that it is done in the context of support. You provide this context by helping your companion remain totally relaxed and quiet.

The Four Activities

The desensitization strategy demands your involvement in four distinct training activities with your companion:

1. Mastering relaxation training

2. Identifying very specific behavioral targets and longer-term attainable goals

3. For each target, constructing a hierarchy of ever-increasing aversive or scary stimuli, from no aversion to extremely aversive or frightening

4. Presenting the hierarchy while pairing a relaxation response with each stimulus.

You may also be called on to coach your companion in honing his or her visualization skills, and to help prevent relapse as your companion recovers.

To prepare for this process, you and your companion should read chapters 4 and 5 so that you both know what's about to take place. Your companion should be able to conceptualize how it works, especially how the learned relaxation indeed blocks the fear and anxiety that can lead to panic attacks. If your companion has trouble conceptualizing the hierarchical presentation, describe the procedure as something akin to climbing a staircase: the steps will be gradual and equal in size.

Get a Target

Write down a target activity that you both want your companion to eventually complete. Pick one that you listed in chapter 5. It could be something like driving beyond a certain boundary, running an errand alone, or walking around the block.

Now you and your companion will create a hierarchy of activity that includes twenty or more steps, each of which provokes a just-noticeable increase in anxiety, according to your companion. If your companion seems to be pretty relaxed while you're doing this activity, it may be that he or she is either getting better or is unable to visualize the scenes you're presenting. There should be at least some mild discomfort (level 2) during the hierarchy development.

When my own clients struggle with visualization, I'm never quite sure whether they're resistant to the process or if, in fact, they can't visualize. Under these circumstances, I suggest to my clients that any visualization activity should be like daydreaming, or like watching a movie in your head. When I engaged Dan in this activity, I reached out and put my hand on his forehead so he could remind himself that he was watching a movie in his head. I had to do this because the desensitization hierarchy didn't seem to bother him as much as I thought it should, even when I put in more aversive stimuli. If you're still unsure whether your companion has experienced the visual images you're presenting, you might say, "Signal me with your left index finger when you have the picture in your head."

Develop the Hierarchy

I want to suggest two ways of creating a hierarchy. The first is the simplest and will include numbered steps from 1 to at least 20. The second method is to construct a narrative passage that begins with a pleasant background. Gradually, more fearsome stimuli are added to the scene. After you develop it, you'll read the passage slowly to your companion. Then your companion should read it alone. Finally, you'll want your companion to read it into a tape recorder so that it can be played back at different practice times during the day. If it's done well, it'll have a sort of hypnotic effect, effectively pairing the aversive stimuli with relaxation.

So if your companion has mastered at least one of the relaxation strategies, you should start building a hierarchy for your first target. I'll give you a sample here that's a common one for an agoraphobe: taking a walk around the block in the middle of the day. I've deliberately made it longer than twenty steps so that you can see how to create very minor, just noticeable differences in aversive stimuli.

1. Sitting at home thinking about a walk outside

2. Getting up and going to the door to take a walk

3. Putting a hand on the doorknob

4. Opening the door

5. Feeling the outside air

6. Taking one step outside the door

7. Taking another step outside the door

8. Walking one yard from the door

9. Walking two yards from the door

10. Walking ten yards from the door

11. Arriving at the main sidewalk

12. Deciding which direction to walk in

13. Taking the first step along the main sidewalk

14. Taking another step along the main sidewalk

15. Walking ten yards along the main sidewalk

16. Walking twenty yards along the main sidewalk

17. Walking fifty yards along the main sidewalk

18. Being on the sidewalk and not being able to see your home

19. Making the turn at the corner so that you're no longer on your street

20. Walking down the adjoining street

21. Walking to the end of the block of the adjoining street

22. Making the turn onto the street that is in the back of your home

23. Meeting a person on the street who says hello

24. Walking to the end of the street

25. Making the turn onto the adjoining street.

26. Meeting two old neighbors who want to know where you've been

27. Having a conversation with the neighbors

28. Continuing on to the end of the street

29. Making the turn onto your own street

30. Returning home

When your companion can go through a hierarchy like this in a completely relaxed fashion, truly visualizing each step, you'll want to begin developing more hierarchies for your selected targets. Remember that the keys to this activity are the gradations between the stimuli and your companion's proficiency in relaxing.

Develop the Story

Try to develop a narrative of the same material. The following is a model of such a story:

I want you to sit there just like that and become very relaxed and comfortable, with a feeling of overwhelming peace and balance. Your muscles are nicely relaxed, and as my voice gradually deepens, you'll find that you will become even more deeply relaxed and feel almost like you're about to go to sleep, just like you did last night. So, as you maintain that warm comfort, just like you're going to sleep in your own bed, you're becoming aware of how much you want to take just a little walk outside, in that pleasant afternoon air that's so warm and comfortable.

Go ahead now and let your mind's eye take you on that little journey. While you're here with me, you're also going to be out there, in your mind. Now that you're completely relaxed and in balance, you find that you're beginning to take that walk in your own mind's eye. Go right on, just like that. You get up from your chair and you go to that front door, and today it seems to be so colorful to look at. That front door is a refreshing opening to something that you haven't experienced for a little while now.

You put your hand on the doorknob and open the door. The fresh, slightly warm air of the afternoon with all of its pleasantness enters your consciousness. That's right, just like that. And now you're finding that standing in the doorway, you're becoming even more relaxed and comfortable and experiencing more of the balance that you want to achieve in your life.

You take just a little step through the door way, then you walk outside. The day, in all its glistening, seems so safe. You begin your pilgrimage with one step in front of another, walking slowly and comfortably, and with balance and unusual strength in your legs and your feet. You feel one foot moving past the other as you continue your stroll. Familiar relaxation moves from your nose to your toes. You reach the sidewalk and decide which way to turn. You let yourself breathe from your belly as you continue to walk slowly, and with tranquility and a feeling of strength. You hardly notice that your home is out of sight as you continue on with your journey. You arrive at the end of the familiar block, and even though you still want to go straight on, you make the turn. Just once around the block today, that's all you'll need to do. That's right. Just like that.

You continue to the end of that block enjoying seeing the other people. Then you make the turn onto the street that's in the back of your own familiar home. You can look over there and feel its presence. And as you do this you're aware that someone is approaching you with a welcoming smile. You acknowledge the smile with a friendly "hello" and a nod. You walk on to the end of the block. You make the turn, even though you want to go on because the warm, soft smells of the day are so entirely different from what you've experienced at home.

Everything's lovely. You continue on, and then two old acquaintances meet up with you. They are very open and excited to see you. You feel like you've been away from them for such a long time. You want to talk to them. And you do, with animation and ease. Then, you're able to easily excuse yourself and travel to the end of the block and to make another turn down your own very familiar street. You continue on blithely, step by step, until you notice that your very own home is in sight. You're very comfortable and cherish this moment. You arrive in front of your home and make the turn toward that door there that you haven't seen for a while. And you're home with a feeling of joy at your accomplishment.

Present the Hierarchy

Start by creating a very tranquil, comfortable mood with your companion's favorite relaxation exercise. You may also help increase his or her calmness by reading a particularly relaxing passage from a book, poem, or spiritual text before beginning desensitization exercises.

In any case, your companion should be completely relaxed before you verbally present a hierarchy. I have my clients relax in a large easy chair in my office. They take three to five minutes to relax and, after checking that they're ready, I begin the hierarchical presentation. If at any time they feel any hint of anxiety (from level 1 up), I ask them to raise their right index finger to signal me that they need to stop. Then I retreat a few steps in the hierarchy, practice more relaxation exercises (even a simple diaphragmatic breath can ease the tension) until they are at least back to level 1, and then I begin presenting again. I try to spend about twenty minutes in the activity and I plan to have them do this with me for approximately five sessions. Some of my colleagues present each of the visual stimuli twice before moving on. You could try that technique if it feels more comfortable to you, although I usually stay with just one presentation.

If the anxiety level zooms up to a four or five, then you need to put more time into relaxation practice before you try it again. And you may need to make smaller steps in the hierarchy than the ones you've developed.

The Next Step

Both of these techniques, the hierarchy and the narrative, can work in very powerful ways, as long as your companion practices. Bear in mind that, as successful as your companion gets with this, it's only the first stage in lowering his or her anxiety enough to return to the outside world and confront those previously feared situations. You may find that before your companion can practice going outside, he or she will need to learn and practice some motivational phrases like "My hyperawareness let's me see the beauty around me," "The map in my head let's me know where I am," or "I'm a road cat."

Preventing Relapse

You'll naturally want to try to prevent too much relapse in your companion's activities. Relapse can interfere with recovery, but it's usually not entirely devastating. In fact, your companion will probably need to learn to live with the ever-present possibility of relapse. You can reassure your companion that the probability of relapse is certainly lessened with relaxation training. If he or she happens to feel a relapse coming on, your companion should have the resources to prevent a full panic attack.

Flooding

As you may recall from chapter 4, flooding is a procedure wherein aversive stimuli are presented rapidly and continuously. The idea is that, with the rapid presentation, anxiety will heighten, peak, and then dissipate, and the aversive stimuli will lose their potency. An analogy is watching a scary movie: The first time you watch, it might terrify you. But if you see it over and over again, you become desensitized, because the surprises are gone.

Here is an easy way to try flooding. Have your companion sit in a comfortable chair. Practice relaxation or not; that's up to you. Now read the previous walk-around-the-block hierarchy items to your companion. But read each item five times before proceeding on to the next item; thus, you will present 150 statements in all. Regardless of how anxious your companion becomes, keep on reading the items, five times each. Don't stop or pause to relax and refresh.

I've said earlier that this technique is not for everyone, and if you and your companion feel that it's just not in the cards, then don't proceed. However, it's powerful, and I've found it to be very successful in treating not only agoraphobia but other anxiety disorders as well.

You might also use the narrative story. Edit out the relaxation statements and then read the narrative rapidly, over and over, five times.

When you have successfully used the desensitization hierarchy for one target, it's time for the two of you to reexamine which of the other targets you want to reach, in what order, and when. Use your list from chapter 5. Map out a schedule of goals you'll work toward with hierarchies or flooding over the next several weeks. Now you have a plan.

Rapid Extinction with Exposure and Immersion

Once your companion has mastered several hierarchies, it's time to venture into the real world. You or your companion might feel more than a trifle wary about this, and that's to be expected. Just try not to lose your momentum. Immersion is really just a new version of the previous, successful visualization activity. If your companion can go outside the home in his or her head and stay relaxed, believe that it is possible to do it for real.

Work Gradually

You can use a hierarchy for exposure and immersion just as you did for the visualization. If, for example, your companion is practicing to walk around the block, try this: The first time your companion tries to walk around the block, you go, too. Thereafter, vary this approach. For instance, walk for the first half of the block, and then let your companion go on alone. Or walk the first half of the block and let your companion go on alone, but say that you'll walk the other way and meet your companion on the street in the back of the home. Then, you'll walk home together. Whatever you do is certainly up to you two to decide. But choose variations that make the exercise doable. Successful completion is crucial.

If these suggestions create a lot of anxiety, try to help your companion practice more relaxation strategies. Also, use a signal system during the work. If you get a signal from your companion to stop and back up, do so. Relax, and proceed again. If continuing appears to be too much for your companion, try modeling and role playing to ease the anxiety, then return to the real-life immersion exercise.

Modeling

Modeling, or viewing how different people take on an experience like walking around the block, can be used to help your companion reduce fears. It can help your companion feel that he or she can be as powerful as others who have felt very anxious. For example, watching quiz show contestants on television can allow your companion to see how people respond when they're under some duress. Point out how the contestants are able to get through the half hour without totally freaking out, even if they're humiliating themselves.

A good "walking" film is *High Noon* with Gary Cooper as the quintessential "man alone," striding to a shootout where he's outnumbered. Your companion could take on a Gary Cooper–type persona as he or she walks around the neighborhood block.

If your companion is able to get out of the house with some help from you, and you're looking for some real-life models, you might want to check out any local meetings of TERRAP (Territorial Apprehensiveness) or NAMI (National Alliance of the Mentally Ill). These are organizations where people can offer your companion support by telling their stories and serving as role models.

Play Roles

In an earlier chapter, I mentioned role playing. This too can be an intermediary step before getting into actual, real-life immersion. Role playing emerged from a psychotherapeutic technique called psychodrama, which was developed in Vienna, by Jacob Moreno between 1910 and 1930. He noticed that people who play nonscripted and unrehearsed parts often experience a certain release of emotional tension when they act out different roles. Your companion might make an imaginary walk through some of the more tormenting stimuli in his or her life this way.

Since you've already decided upon targets together, try to work toward one of the targets using role playing. You can create a whole sequence of roles and scenes around the target behavior. You may find that role playing works even better than the visual desensitization hierarchy. Following are some good role playing techniques.

Make a Scene. Before starting, your companion should engage in some of the basic relaxation practices. Then, your companion should spend a few minutes creating a scene that is related to one of the target goals. When the scene is created, he or she can act it out.

Body Sculpting. To prevent a wobbly start to the role play, your companion can create a personal "body sculpture" to express what he or she is currently feeling. While thinking about accomplishing the target goal, your companion should show the tension and exertion of venturing toward the completion of this goal. Does your companion's face and body reflect his or her fear? It might help if your companion looks at pictures of human sculptures and then assumes an expressive pose.

Use a Soliloquy. After the sculpting technique, your companion can develop a soliloquy, or monologue, about what he or she is about to encounter. This can be passive, humorous, or dramatic. Consider using the hierarchy about the outdoors. The point of the soliloquy is for your companion to explore his or her thoughts and feelings.

Develop a Monodrama. Now your companion may create a monodrama, or narrative, of, say, actually walking through the neighborhood. The difference between the soliloquy and the monodrama is that, in the monodrama, your companion describes not only his or her thoughts and feelings, but also the environment, the action, and even the other characters in the scene. He or she can make the scene ever more detailed, expressing all of the fears and inhibitions that seem to be keeping him or her confined to the home. When your companion encounters another person, you could, if your companion wanted, join in and play a part that your companion scripts for you.

Role Reversal. Finally, after you observe all of this, you and your companion should switch roles. You can play your companion's role, and your companion can either watch or take on any of the roles that have been created by you. This is *role reversal,* and it offers you a terrific opportunity to feel what it's like to be in your companion's shoes. You'll mirror your companion, so he or she will see what he or she looks and talks like while simulating these different experiences.

Continuing Real-Life Practice

After working through these psychodramas, your companion may be ready for real-life immersion. Now, I've already mentioned that the most effective technique of all is real-life confrontation with the feared stimuli. The procedure for immersion is similar to that for activities described so far: sharpening relaxation skills, agreeing on a target, breaking the target down into small steps, and approaching the event calmly yet boldly. Preparing for and practicing immersion will probably be more time consuming for you.

Your companion will need to stay in "relaxation conditioning," practicing his or her chosen exercises regularly. You'll need to be available as a motivator, listener, confidant, counselor, and coach.

Review your recovery plan and choose an appropriate immersion target. You can spend a few days on this if you like. Work with a therapist if you need to. Be aware that if your companion has any reluctance about giving up the phobia, it will come out here.

When you try real-life immersion, let it be okay for your companion to feel a fair amount of anxiety. In the imagery desensitization, I recommended that you keep your companion's level at 1 or below. But in the real-life experience, let it go to as high as 3 before you have your companion back up, relax, and try again.

Psychologists have known for quite a while that there is a complex relationship between performance and fear: either too much fear or too little fear can adversely affect performance. But it's possible to achieve an optimal level of stimulation or fear. With this optimal level, performance can be enhanced. So hold on to this thought and let the anxiety level rise up as you practice the real-life techniques. If your companion has a few stomach butterflies as you go through the practice, that's good.

To summarize your role: you are the coach. It's absolutely essential that you help prepare your companion for the activities that you're going to embark on together. Lack of preparation or the inability to quickly create deep relaxation is going to inhibit this whole process from working well.

Be sure also that the target selection is appropriate and that the imagined or real-life steps or gradations represent equally difficult intervals of activity; this lets your companion train for the long haul. Also, be sure that the gradations are related to real-life events. For example, don't create a hierarchy where a lion or tiger is going to jump out from between tall buildings!

Be Realistic

Both of you must try to be realistic about the immersion process. Don't rush it. Let it unfold gradually. If you move along too quickly, your companion's confidence is going to be blown and the setback may keep him or her from beginning again, or worse, even from continuing to practice the relaxation exercises that are such an important part of all of this.

Don't Expect the Worst

If your companion has some degree of struggle with any of the recovery activities you try together, don't expect the worst. You will get both yourself and your companion into real hot water if you're just waiting for a disaster. Focus your attention instead on the work itself, and keep the faith that recovery will come. And if at any time you do not feel that your companion is ready for a particular challenge, then be sure to say so and to explain what you think needs to happen before you two take it on.

Reading Body Signals

Now you have learned about a series of techniques that are known to be highly effective in treating agoraphobia. But one of the issues that people with panic disorder and agoraphobia have in common is the fear that they are going to have a panic attack when an internal signal tells them that an attack is about to begin. I'll now describe some techniques that can keep your companion going through the more demanding real-life desensitization and help him or her practice despite higher anxiety levels. The following strategies allow your companion to react in appropriate and nonfearful ways in the face of fear signals: applied tension, anxiety management training (AMT), and interoceptive exposure and deconditioning.

Applied Tension

After all of your efforts at mastering relaxation techniques, I'm going to shift gears for a moment and suggest the opposite: a tension building technique. Here's why. I suspect that your companion may have a terribly difficult time handling some of the practice techniques and real-life exposure alone because he or she is afraid of passing out in public. Dan had a difficult time coping with this fear. Though he is a highly functioning executive now, to the present day his greatest fear is the humiliation he will feel if he passes out at some inopportune time.

I have found that the technique called *applied tension* can be a "quick fix" for anyone who fears passing out or having a panic attack in public. In this technique, your companion quickly tenses the facial muscles, along with other muscles in the hands, thighs, feet, and stomach. It resembles the clenching part of the Jacobsonian progressive muscle relaxation technique, though in this case it's done much more rapidly and it doesn't necessarily go in order from your nose to your toes.

The technique makes your companion's body begin to feel slightly warmer—a sign of relaxation. I've developed a variation on the applied tension technique that I've found very effective for eliminating the fear of fainting in public places. I have my most "fainting fearful" clients press their thumb into the fleshy space between their opposite thumb and index finger. Try it yourself. You should apply a reasonably strong pressure that causes a slight degree of pain. You can do this very quickly; it takes only a second or two and can be done anywhere and any time. I have taught this technique to anxious job seekers for years and they have told me that when they use it, it feels as if they have just taken a brief whiff of smelling salts.

Anxiety Management Training

Anxiety management training (AMT) is a technique developed by Suinn and Richardson (1971) that can be very useful in helping your companion identify the internal signs that lead to either the onset of a panic attack or the fear of a panic attack. In this technique, your companion recalls the experience of a panic attack or the fear of a panic attack and describes how it felt. Your companion should both pay attention to these symptoms in an unafraid way and also feel as if he or she can exert some degree of control over them. In a sense, your companion is learning to take some degree of responsibility for the symptoms. So what your companion learns to do is to recognize the symptoms of a fear response or panic attack and then mobilize a response to this through well-practiced relaxation techniques that confront, reduce, and then eliminate the panic symptoms.

These are the steps your companion can use to practice AMT. You can serve as coach and trainer in the process.

1. Have your companion become proficient at relaxation training.

2. Have your companion list the very worst panic attacks that he or she has ever had. If the attack was recent, have him or her describe in vivid detail all of the body reactions. Now, have your companion write down a clear description of the scenes. Be sure he or she includes the circumstances, like the location and time of day and year, and any details that can reproduce the anxiety. Your

companion should feel anxiety at a level of 5 when experiencing this scene. If possible, the scene should be a public one from which escape was impossible. If your companion did escape, this exercise will not work nearly as well. (In the film *Finding Forrester*, Forrester's panic attack in Penn Station in New York is a good model.) An escape response gives your companion an inappropriate solution and that's why it's better not to use it for this exercise.

Most agorophobes remember several dramatic scenes that can still create anxiety. Pick five of these scenes and rank them in order of panic production. The least scary should get a one and the most scary should have a five. Now for the next few days, take your companion through the next three steps (3, 4, 5) with each of the panic-producing scenes.

3. Help your companion become completely relaxed. When he or she has signaled you that the panic level is 0 or 1, start reading material that you've put together from the descriptions of the first panic-eliciting scene.

Gradually your companion should move from an anxiety level of 1 to an anxiety level of 5. Use the right index finger–raising signal, in which you will probably be well practiced by this point.

4. When the anxiety is going full blast, ask your companion to tune into the body sensations he or she is experiencing, such as tensions, changes in sweating or heart rate, or jitteriness. Ask your companion to make mental notes of all of the symptoms, but without losing the visual image. Try to keep the image powerful and the anxiety level high.

5. Now, your companion should move back toward a state of high relaxation and balanced muscle tone using any of the relaxation techniques that work best. You might also try to develop some relaxing visualizations for this part of the exercise. Practice the whole sequence repeatedly over the course of several days, until your companion can switch on the relaxation response very quickly when the anxiety-producing scene is presented.

AMT will help your companion have some degree of control over the progression of anxiety symptoms into a full-fledged panic attack. This will empower him or her to take even further risks in the recovery process.

Interoceptive Exposure and Deconditioning

In the sense that agoraphobia is the fear of fear and that what needs to eliminated is the fear response, this next technique may be among the most powerful. It deals even more specifically with panic's internal body cues than either applied tension or AMT. When we're afraid, we are all usually aware of changes in our bodies, and the increased awareness that we're afraid in turn increases the fear. Imagine if you could change your response to these cues from increased fear to relaxation. *Interoceptive exposure and deconditioning,* developed by Zuercher-White (1998), is designed to do just that. It's a very nice step beyond the AMT technique.

Zuercher-White is quite correct when she posits that the greater we fear the physical sensations of panic, the more frequently we tend to look for signs of panic. We become hypervigilant. (Agoraphobes are known for their hypervigilance.) This hypervigilance to internal cues is used in AMT. Interoceptive exposure goes further in that it simultaneously exposes a person like your companion to internal panic cues from which there is no escape while demonstrating that these internal cues, these sensations of panic, are harmless.

This technique is fairly straightforward and easy to practice with your companion. Some cognitive components you can add to the work will be discussed in the next section. But try the basic, behavioral technique first. You're going to create a whole host of paniclike symptoms while in the safety of your companion's home. There'll be no escape.

There are a few cautions to take before you begin. These exercises, should be done without using any medication, especially the BZs. These exercises will work best if your companion can feel the full discomfort of the internal cues. According to Zuercher-White your companion should not partake of these exercises if he or she has a seizure disorder, serious asthma, chronic arrythmia, heart or lung problems, fainting spells and/or very low blood pressure, or happens to be pregnant. Further, she recommends consulting with your physician about the technique before trying it.

To begin the work, have your companion pick out the panic symptoms that he or she fears the most and that seem to elicit either panic attacks or fear of panic attacks. The checklist below may help.

_____ Chest pains

_____ Choking sensations

_____ Cold sweat

_____ Difficulty seeing

_____ Dizziness

_____ Feeling faint

_____ Hyperventilation

____ Numbness

____ Shortness of breath

____ Stomach butterflies

____ Stomach cramps

____ Tachycardia (rapid heart rate)

____ Thoughts of escape

____ Tightness around your head

____ Tingling

Now you'll begin to develop some exercises that elicit the symptoms on your checklist. Try to choose exercises that will create some of the sensations that are the most pernicious for your companion. As the caregiver, you can model the exercises for your companion.

You can help your companion to feel comfortable during the exercise with strong coaching. Don't push too hard. On the familiar 0 to 5 anxiety scale, try to keep them at a level no higher than 3 so that your companion keeps some feeling of control. Zuercher-White warns that your companion must distinguish between the anxiety that is produced by the exercise, or sensation anxiety, and real fear. Fear can come from the sensations, but the sensations can be produced without fear, and that is what you're shooting for. As your companion practices, he or she should begin to feel a moderate degree of comfort and relaxation. But if a panic attack starts seeming possible, have your companion stop the particular exercise and practice diaphragmatic breathing or another relaxation exercise.

Most exercises last for twenty to thirty seconds; some may be tried longer. I'll give a suggested time for each. You may double the time in those circumstances where you both feel that your companion could use more of a challenge—that is, if the comfort level your companion happens to be experiencing is too high.

Following are some exercise ideas. Be aware that there is no guarantee that these exercises will produce exactly the same sensations others have had. They should work in most circumstances, though, and they are useful to try. Some of the suggestions come from Zuercher-White and some are from my own experience.

Chest Pains. Have your companion sit in a chair with eyes closed. Then place your thumb on his or her solar plexus and push in for twenty seconds. Then release. Your companion may also hold a magazine against his or her chest while you press. My clients report that this technique makes the pain seem to spread over a wider area.

Choking Sensations. Place your thumb on your companion's throat and slowly apply increasing pressure. Have your companion try to swallow regularly during this time.

Increase the pressure for thirty seconds and then hold at a constant pressure for sixty seconds.

Cold Sweat. Have your companion dress in a turtleneck, sweater, overcoat, hat, and scarf. You might also place a very warm heating pad on his or her lap. For the next two minutes, have your companion imagine being lost in an urban wilderness, unable to find a safe place.

Difficulty Seeing. Have your companion blink very rapidly for twenty seconds and then focus on some object outside a window. Repeat this four times.

Dizziness. Spin your companion slowly with eyes shut for thirty seconds. Have your companion open the eyes and try to focus. Repeat this one more time.

Feeling Faint. Have your companion sit in a chair and then bend the head over between the legs, lower than the heart, and hold it there for one minute. Then after one minute, prompt him or her to quickly lift the head, stand up, and walk around. You may also have your companion kneel on the floor for two minutes and then rise quickly, standing up and walking around.

Hyperventilation. Have your companion breathe deeply and rapidly through the mouth for one minute.

Numbness. While sitting, your companion should clench both fists and tighten the chest, thighs, and calves—basically tensing the whole body. Have your companion continue to breathe deeply for ninety seconds, while he or she no longer seems to have much feeling in the body. (As noted previously, this is a nice demonstration of how we develop stress-related problems by holding the tension in our bodies.)

Shortness of Breath. Have your companion breathe through a straw for two minutes. Repeat this with you pinching the straw slightly so that breathing is more difficult.

Stomach Butterflies. Have your companion sit in a straight chair, lean back slightly, and then tense the stomach muscles as if about to begin a sit-up. He or she should hold this for thirty seconds before releasing the tension and noticing the feeling in the stomach.

Stomach Cramps. Make a fist and push it into your companion's stomach. Hold it there for thirty seconds.

Tachycardia. Have your companion jog in place vigorously for ninety seconds and then immediately sit down.

Tightness around the Head. Tie a scarf or bandanna tightly around your companion's head and leave it there for thirty seconds.

Tingling. Have your companion lie on the ground, head propped up with one hand, for five minutes. Have him or her release the position and feel the tingling in the arm, like it's gone to sleep.

You can certainly work with your companion to try any number of variations on these themes. The point is to ensure that your companion has the aversive internal cue. When this happens, record the physical experiences that your companion says he or she is having, especially any that are fear-related. Then repeat the interoceptive cue exercise a second time. But now, have your companion restore balance to the body by immediately engaging in a relaxation technique. In this way, your companion learns to combat body experiences with other body experiences.

When your companion has achieved a degree of proficiency working with you in this area, suggest that he or she try it alone. Knowing how to use this tool can help him or her feel comfortable in the more demanding real-life desensitization activities, like going to the grocery store or walking around the block.

Up until this point, the strategies in this chapter have all used predominately behavioral work like heavy doses of desensitization. We now move on to the cognitive and cognitive behavioral approaches.

Cognitive Treatments

In chapter 4, I talked about some of the thoughts people have that can have a deleterious impact on their behavior. These thoughts mostly have to do with misguided assumptions people make about the world. The first of the cognitive approaches I'll describe involves trying to restructure your companion's expectations in a rational manner that will lead to a more positive outlook.

Change Negative Expectations

In cognitive work, one of the goals for your companion is to change negative expectations—to assume that good things rather than bad ones are going to happen. So rather than focusing upon what's wrong, your work with your companion is to focus upon what's right with your companion, the family, the community, and the world.

When Dan was to return to work, his expectation was that people would ask a lot of personal questions about where he had been and what had gone wrong. Dan regarded such questions as negative and intrusive. I spent some time with him trying to have him frame this expectation differently. I had Dan confront his negative expectations and pursue more rational, upbeat thoughts of what would happen when he returned to work. I had him consider that:

Most would not have noticed his absence.

All would welcome him back.

His employer would want him to get to work.

There would be more concern about his productivity than his personality.

His personal problems were not of much concern to the people at work.

Everyone has personal problems; Dan was not special.

He still had the capacity to work well, to respect the people around him, and to be thoughtful, creative, and kind to other people.

This cognitive approach gave Dan the important message that he could return to work and engage in productive practices.

Using this technique can help your companion develop a much more positive perspective about what he or she will be able to do. Practice the following exercises:

1. Help your companion develop positive visualizations of success in his or her recovery exercises.

2. Keep your messages to each other about the practice activities upbeat and positive. For example, when something doesn't go so well, rather than telling each other it'll never get better, say and believe that this may just take a little longer than had been expected.

3. Encourage your companion to use the extra time on his or her hands, to engage in positive activities, including more reading about the disorder and finding more role models in books and on film. Such reading and viewing can include inspirational stories of people who have found interest and peace in overcoming some of the difficult dilemmas of life.

4. Your companion can keep a journal of positive thoughts and feelings. My client John kept two journals: an anger journal and a journal of activities he was grateful for and proud of.

5. Help your companion exercise, practice relaxation, and live more mindfully. That includes eliminating those parts of his or her diet that could be causing more anxiety, like sugar and caffeine, for instance. You and your companion can also both listen to more music or sit in lounge chairs in the backyard—enjoy the little things.

Get Rid of Illogical Thoughts

As you've read earlier, in chapter 4, anxiety problems can stem from illogical thoughts and beliefs. So help your companion consider two issues. The first is that thoughts and assumptions about how the world works can affect how he or she experiences life emotionally. Second, your companion needs to recognize where his or her thinking is just plain wrong.

Errors in Logic Checklist

Using Beck's approach (1987), I point out the errors in logic my agoraphobic clients have. Similarly, both you and your companion should identify what errors in logic seem to drive your companion's thoughts and ultimately his or her behavior. Photocopy this checklist so that both you and your companion can fill out a copy. (You will both be identifying your companion's behaviors.)

_____ Arriving at conclusions without any real, hard evidence

_____ Focusing on insignificant details of life while ignoring important ones

_____ Developing conclusions from data gathered from a single experience

_____ Making a mountain from a molehill

_____ Minimizing the good things about life

_____ Taking responsibility for events over which you had no control

_____ Viewing life as all-or-nothing, black and white, good and evil

_____ Filtering in negative information, filtering out the positive

_____ Believing that what you feel must be real

_____ Concerning yourself only with what you "should" do

How do your lists compare? You might use the checklist to help your companion make worldview changes and simply feel better about himself or herself.

Get Rid of Irrational Beliefs

Beck studies errors in logic. Albert Ellis, on the other hand, focuses upon beliefs that he felt were irrational. He thinks that most irrational beliefs are based on expectations inculcated by parents. Where Beck might try to logically confront the inappropriate thoughts, Ellis believes that it's the destructive beliefs that must be aggressively confronted. Only then can you help someone address his or her family expectations and start overcoming some of his or her life issues and disorders.

I asked Susie, a new agoraphobe I've been treating, to describe to me why she could no longer go to work. She said that was simple. She was afraid that she was going to have a heart attack on the highway and that she would either die, have an accident, or be put into an insane asylum (her words) for trying to drive in her disordered state of body and mind. I used Ellis' approach to break down Susie's irrational belief.

According to Ellis you can create an *ABCD list* of information to break down a problem to its kernels and then refute it, like this:

A. You experience an upsetting external event.

B. You create a distorted belief about the event.

C. You develop a possible consequence of this belief.

D. You dispute the belief.

Here is one of Susie's lists:

A. I've got to drive to my nerve-wracking job.

B. I'll be thinking about some employee confrontation and I'll have a heart attack.

C. I'll die, have an accident, or be institutionalized.

D. I am in great physical shape and have low cholesterol, low blood pressure, and no genetic history of heart trouble. I won't have a heart attack. My nerve-wracking job won't give me a heart attack. Gee whiz, it hasn't even caused an increase in my blood pressure.

Breaking her distorted beliefs into Ellis' ABCDs is very helpful for Susie, although she is very creative at constructing further irrational beliefs. But understanding, confronting, and disputing these beliefs has already been useful in her work toward recovery.

Let's see how this might work using the earlier example of a walk in the neighborhood.

A. I'm taking a walk into the neighborhood, something I haven't done in a while.

B. I'll run into someone who wants to talk to me and I'll have a panic attack or a heart attack.

C. No one will be able to help me and the ambulance will come and I'll be taken to a hospital where I will die or be forgotten. I'll have had a stroke or a heart attack, so I won't be able to communicate.

D. I might have a panic attack. But I will be able to point and tell someone where I live. I am at no risk for a stroke or heart attack.

Let's do another:

A. I'm having lunch with a friend in a restaurant.

B. I'm afraid I will choke on my food and not be able to breathe.

C. I will black out or I'll stick my fingers down my throat to stop the choking. I'll be unconscious regardless and people in the restaurant will think I'm dying. I will never be allowed in there again. I would rather die than be humiliated like this.

D. I won't choke. I have never choked. If I do choke, I'll take a drink. I know that every restaurant has someone who is educated in the Heimlich maneuver. My friend will summon a person to help me.

Now all of this seems simple enough that you should be able to use the ABCDs to help your companion ferret out all his or her irrational beliefs. So why hasn't this technique proven to be universally effective? The problem is that all of these irrational thoughts are also automatic, and even subtle changes will make them feel like new beliefs. They will always reappear for your companion to argue with.

Part of what you can help your companion do is discover the automatic thoughts that he or she uses to keep from engaging in a stronger, more rapid recovery. You need to know what the thoughts are, when they occur, and what seem to be the consequences. Then you need to help your companion develop strategies to dispute the thoughts.

Note that these thoughts are almost like the classically conditioned response described in chapter 4. There's a trigger, and then immediately there is a response in the form of a belief. These negative thoughts or beliefs need to be confronted and disputed. You'll find that most of the beliefs involve errors of logic like those on the checklist you and your companion completed earlier. For example, you'll find that your companion will have exaggerated ideas about what will become of him or her, or engage in black and white, all-or-nothing thinking. These scary, distorted thoughts will prompt your companion to try to find ways of being in control. For your companion, the ultimate control is staying home. Your work as a coach is to try to motivate your companion to put together lists of triggers, irrational beliefs, and the horrific consequences that will ensue, then to help him or her dispute both the belief and the imagined consequences. You may be able to dispute the belief and then there will be no worry about the consequences. Encourage your companion to track progress in a journal, using five columns like these.

Date	Trigger	Belief	Consequence	Dispute

Your companion's work will require talking without fear of embarrassment about why a particular belief is irrational. Your support and positive response can help a lot. In addition, he or she will need to learn to stop thoughts that are clearly irrational. I have some of my clients regularly wear a rubber band around their wrists and when they have a trigger that leads to an irrational belief, they're to snap the rubber band. The snapping is a distraction so that the person never even gets to the consequence of the belief. But the snapping also seems to help to eliminate irrational thinking altogether. My clients report that they eliminate 30 percent of their irrational thoughts in the first week of using this technique. They're often amazed at how much of their operating was affected by irrational thinking and beliefs.

Clients have also had some degree of success simply yelling "STOP" to themselves, either out loud or in their heads. This, like the snapping of the rubber band, seems to help eliminate irrational beliefs.

Having my clients talk into a tape recorder about some of their beliefs and their own rationale for those beliefs seems to help them see how nutty the beliefs and their imagined consequences are. Clients have recorded their irrational beliefs and thoughts when on the verge of a panic attack, and when they came to my office to play back the recording, they laughed loudly about what they were saying. It helped them to hear me laugh right along with them. They were able to dispute their own behavior because when they heard it played back it sounded silly to them.

Another useful trick my clients use is to carry some three-by-five index cards with them. When they feel that a trigger has occurred that is eliciting an irrational belief, they write it down. Later they can make a recording of the trigger, belief, consequence, and disputation and share it with me.

Your companion can use any of these techniques I've described to get some greater degree of mindfulness and conscious control over the entire process.

Cognitive Behavioral Approaches

At this point, you have been introduced to most of the techniques you'll need to help your companion cope. But these techniques will be most effective if you integrate them into a combined, cognitive behavioral approach. Such an approach has three parts: a conceptual base with which to understand agoraphobia; skills to rehearse and to put into action, including both the behavioral skills and the cognitive skills just discussed; and an integration of understanding with technique.

It goes something like this. You explain the recovery process, using information from this book. You then help your companion develop relaxation skills to use in different forms of desensitization including real-life desensitization or immersion. When your companion begins to have conscious fears that he or she is not progressing quickly enough or that triggers are causing irrational thoughts that interfere with practice, you help him or her confront these.

In the final phase of recovery, you help have your companion begin to change his or her views about the agoraphobia. New language can reframe the entire agoraphobic experience. For example, instead of saying, "I'm a nut," an agoraphobe might say, "I'm a highly sensitive person." Or, an agoraphobe could affirm, "I can read people and situations better than anyone else. I'm always on alert, at the ready."

Stress inoculation training is a cognitive behavioral intervention described by Meichenbaum (1985) that can help your companion try new tasks. First, he or she will need to restructure irrational ideas. Second, he or she should create a problem-solving focus. Let's say, for example, that your companion is about to practice a real-life immersion, and walk around the block. But he or she believes that failure means he or she will never try this again. Your work is to help your companion confront these irrational beliefs by telling him or her that most activities in life do not have "all or none" consequences. You can also help your companion to refrain from jumping to any sort of quick conclusion about what's going to happen. And you can emphasize that he or she doesn't have to be perfect, but just needs to try.

A final integration of the cognitive and behavioral components of walking around the block (or any other target activity) is this: to help your companion realize that what he or she is doing in walking around the block is really just solving a problem. It is not a huge undertaking. Yet it is perfectly permissible to have some feelings of anxiety about it. Help your companion to see the walk around the block as a problem that he or she wants to solve and *can* solve with a plan. Help your companion think back to the resources that he or she has to accomplish the goal, and ahead to the reward he or she will receive upon reaching the goal.

Integration gives your companion a sense of control. The task is no longer simply real-life immersion, but real-life problem solving.

Cognitive behavioral integration has the benefit of helping your companion master coping skills and problem-solving skills. At the same time it helps prevent fear of relapse because the task is no longer about confronting anxiety, but about solving a problem. This reframing takes pressure off your companion while granting him or her some control. You'll find that when you've integrated one immersion episode with a degree of success, then you and your companion have a problem-solving model that you can use again and again.

7

Preventing Victimization and Codependency

Now that you've been through the caregiving exercises, it's time to evaluate your feelings about your many responsibilities. Earlier, in chapter 2 you evaluated whether you needed a stress inoculation. In this chapter, we'll explore two phenomena, victimization and codependency, that can potentially do the most damage to you and to your relationship with your companion.

Victimization

The world is full of victims. The evening news tell us about the victims of crime, poverty, and unemployment. We hear of the victims of historic world events like the Vietnam War or the Holocaust. Earthquakes, floods, and tornados all have their victims, as do relationship abuse, sexual abuse, and neglect. These events yield groups of people who may have the added suffering of a mental disorder, post-traumatic stress disorder (PTSD).

"Victim" is one word you probably never expected to use to describe yourself. But why not? You happen to be an excellent candidate for this disquieting title. You share a commonality with the victims of rape, incest, war, earthquakes, floods, and tornados. Like these victims, your crisis was dropped into your lap. You didn't plan for this caregiving role, you weren't prepared for it by education and experience, and you probably didn't have many people to turn to for help.

To be sure, you don't need to have a traumatic experience to feel like a victim. People feel victimized when the direction of their lives doesn't meet their expectations. They experience psychological loss. Their indignation rises. Victims feel as if they have been treated unfairly or robbed of their life goals. Just ask anyone who has suffered discrimination in employment or housing.

In short, a victim is anyone whose life has been interrupted by some kind of catastrophic event. That probably describes you. Your life has been thrown into disarray. You've not only had to react to this as you would to any other type of disruptive life event, you've also had to reinvent and energize yourself for the role of a caregiver. That role has forced you to take a new look at yourself as you try to determine what kind of caregiver you could become. It's demanded that you take on a whole new set of unfamiliar activities. You've also had to make a choice about whether to learn the new skills involved in coaching someone with a psychological disorder.

Do You Feel Victimized?

If you've been forced to give up a substantial part of your free time and to add more responsibilities to an already busy life, you can feel victimized and hostile. Maybe that hostility is directed at your companion, your family, and those friends and acquaintances who are able to shirk this kind of responsibility. You expect people who are close to you to understand your anger, but they're completely unsympathetic. That adds to your feeling of victimization. You feel doubly burdened, too, because you have to tell your companion what he or she needs to know but not necessarily what he or she wants to hear, which makes you both feel hostility and guilt.

Look again at how you happened upon this role. Was it thrust upon you or did you choose to help out? If you had no choice, maybe you feel trapped. If you did have a choice, maybe you're angry at yourself for not being assertive enough to say no. Conceivably, you could delegate more activities, but you choose not to. Maybe you have trouble asking for help. Could it be, too, that you want all of the credit, especially if your companion recovers under your care?

You have to face the fact that this caregiving experience has been quite a hassle, and that this hassle isn't just a single-season event. Caregiving can consume your time and your life. Your life's interrupted. You have to wait on your companion in different ways.

You're concerned about the cost of the services your companion needs. You can't freely express what you feel. And you worry, both for your companion and for yourself.

The media reports daily that the stress of caregiving, especially caring for the elderly, can affect your mental and physical well-being. You're experiencing not only the overall impact of assuming the caregiving role, but also a major identity shift. You're also experiencing both daily hassles and some lack of personal independence and privacy. Those are the experiences that can cause the greatest amount of life stress, whether you're a caregiver or not. Meanwhile, you've tried to become a coach as well as a companion and caregiver. To do that you've had to absorb a whole new body of knowledge.

As you review your own journal about the caregiving activities, reflect on some of the issues you need to address to care for yourself. Even if you feel like a victim, and even if you are one in some ways, you don't have to be one forever, even with a potential lifetime of caregiving duties.

Emotional Responses to Caregiving

You've probably had a variety of emotional reactions to the caregiving experience, many having to do with the intrusive nature of the experience. You didn't expect this to happen, didn't plan for it, and now, even after all of the work you've done with your companion, you may still resent it.

What are some of the responses that you might be expected to have? Try this checklist.

_____ I'm angry about assuming the role of caregiver.

_____ I'm fearful that my companion won't get any better.

_____ My self-esteem has been affected by the caregiving experience. I'm just not very good at this.

_____ I feel guilty that I can't provide more time and energy for my companion.

_____ I get depressed from time to time over the situation I'm in.

_____ I find that I'm anxious, nervous, and tense over the responsibility I feel.

_____ I've had my own physical health problems since I took on this role.

_____ I've used drugs, alcohol, or prescription medications to help get through this.

_____ I seem to have lost my normally effective social skills.

_____ I'm having troubles in my other relationships.

_____ I seem to have lost my interest in sex.

_____ I sometimes act inappropriately toward others, yelling at them unnecessarily.

_____ My own sense of safety in the world has been altered, perhaps permanently.

_____ I find that from time to time I want to strike out at my companion.

_____ I don't laugh much anymore.

There are some victimlike reactions that you should pay attention to in yourself. These include anger, anxiety, depression, blows to your self-esteem, guilt, and problems with physical health. Note which ones appear to be most prominent for you. Below are some quick mental strategies that can help you move beyond the role of victim.

Acknowledge Your Anger

There will be times when you are angry with the recovery process. That's natural. You may feel anger over your circumstances. You may feel frustrated that your companion is unable or unwilling to do more, to try harder.

When used properly, anger can be a useful emotion. It can keep you away from people and situations that aren't healthy for you. From time to time it can even energize or stimulate you. But you run into serious trouble if your standard mode of operating is one of constant anger. In the end you're not going to get what you want and you may harm your companion. You will also lose some support from those who care about you.

Any good coach, trainer, or caregiver will counsel you to own up to your anger and express it appropriately. If that's too hard for you, as it is for many, then find your own friend or therapist to talk to. It's typical for angry people to displace their anger onto someone else. Your personal work as a caregiver is to make sure that you don't displace your anger onto your companion.

Anger at Impotence

Try to recall a recent event when you became very angry with a situation that you felt you had no control over—maybe a bank transaction, a billing error, or a situation at work. The stimulus got you revved up, but really what you were angry about was your own impotence. What did you do? You may have obsessed some, but then, like most angry people, you wanted to feel that you were at least doing something. If so, you probably acted out a bit. Maybe a friend, companion, spouse, lover, or dog got the brunt of your emotional catharsis.

When you end up taking action, that's unrelated to the event that got you angry in the first place, you can run into trouble. Again, part of your work is to ensure that such anger is not misdirected at your companion.

Don't Distort

If you're feeling victimized, deprived and bewildered, it's important for you to be mindful of some of the information presented earlier on cognitive processing. Creating distortions or irrational ideas about your work as a caregiver is the recipe for keeping you in the victim role. In your role as a caregiving companion, your work is to deal with the real, nondistorted problems that emerge in this situation. So pay attention to any tendency you have to behave in the following ways:

- Evaluating events or facts as worth either everything or nothing

- Jumping to conclusions without careful consideration or consultation

- Forgetting about or discounting all of the good work you've done with your companion

- Taking any criticism from your companion too personally

- Overextending yourself and then becoming angry about having no time to yourself

- Blaming yourself if your companion doesn't get better

If you're persistently doing any of these things it's time for you to be like Sergeant Joe Friday and get "just the facts." Get away from the notion that what you feel must be real. You may find relief in some of the exercises for changing errors in logic and irrational beliefs described in chapter 6.

Evaluate Your Effort

It will help you to be less angry if you can evaluate your effort rather than the outcomes. Recall how much you've learned and how close you've been able to become with your companion. While you're at it, try to look at your concepts of success and failure. If you see your caregiving as either completely successful or completely unsuccessful depending upon the outcome, try to step away from that perspective. You don't know when all of this work will finally come to harvest; it could be years. That is not to say that you'll be the caregiver for all of this time. But some of the work that you're doing today may have an impact months from now. In any event, your work is worthwhile.

Address Your Anxiety

I've talked about anxiety throughout this book, but haven't really addressed yours. If you yourself don't suffer from an anxiety disorder, your anxiety is probably better characterized as objective or realistic anxiety. That is, you feel anxiety in the presence of a real and palpable threat. Your companion's fears are equally real, but are not based on a tangible threat.

Your anxiety might also involve performance anxiety. Parents often feel anxious about a child's school performance because they feel that their worth as parents will be reflected in how well the child does. You may not be the parent of your companion, but you probably want to be the very best coach and caregiver you can be. You don't want to make errors. But you have no training or expertise, and no one to compare yourself to. Your performance anxiety comes from real concerns.

Deal with Feelings of Vulnerability

There are several areas where you may feel vulnerable. One is in the feeling that you don't have the skills for this work. After all, you probably have no formal training. But information is always accessible, and the fact that you're reading this book means you're trying to learn. Using the Internet and reading other books and articles referenced here can help, and support groups are available as well.

You may also feel some anxiety about being rejected. Your companion may get angry with you in your role as a coach and may not want to engage in activities with you. Sometimes, that's just par for the course. You may also feel some rejection and criticism from other family members. Try to see such criticism as expressions of these people's own fears and anxieties. They very likely have nothing to do with how well you're doing as a caregiver. Finally, try not to replay old criticisms from the past. That's old history, and it won't help you in this process.

So what should you do with your anxiety? Use some of the same activities that you're coaching your companion in, especially those that involve relaxation and information gathering. They'll give you the resources to combat your own feelings of anxiety.

Examine Your Depression

Depression is a familiar characteristic of victimization. You may not have a diagnosable form of depression, but you may experience considerable sadness or worry over the predicament that you and your companion share. Maybe your vulnerability and disappointment make you feel more sad than anxious.

Most depression involves some kind of feeling of loss. People are depressed when they lose loved ones, obviously. Loss of employment usually elicits some loneliness and sadness. Any depression or sadness you feel is possibly related to the loss of the lifestyle you were accustomed to. You may feel you've lost your sense of personal power. Your economic circumstances may have changed as a result of your companion's illness.

So what should you do with your own depression or sadness? First, check out your symptoms to see if you're seriously depressed and not just sad. Tune in to your appetite: Is it much more or less than it used to be? Are you tired all the time? Do you want to sleep all the time or not at all? Are you more irritable or moody? Listen to what others (not your companion) tell you about this. Do you lack energy for or an interest in the other activities of your life? Do you keep up with habitual activities like washing the dishes, or are there stacks of pots, pans, dishes, and silverware that haven't been attended to? Pay attention to any physical changes like headaches and abdominal cramps, and to any increase in your use of alcohol or prescription medications.

If you're experiencing any of the above symptoms you may be clinically depressed, and you need to take some measures to care for yourself. Tell a professional—a therapist or physician—what you're going through, and ask for help. There are some behavioral and cognitive techniques you can use to help pull yourself out of the pit, whether you're clinically depressed or just feeling blue. Some of these will sound familiar to you.

1. Keep a record of your symptoms and behavior.

2. Keep note of your accomplishments in caregiving and other areas of your life.

3. Look for any twists in your own thought pattern that seem to pound you down emotionally. Maybe you think you should have tried harder or been a more empathetic coach. Those thoughts are harsh, and won't help the situation.

4. Confront your feelings of helplessness. Just like your companion is doing, break your recovery into little steps and reward yourself for your own good thoughts. You've coached your companion on the ABCDs of irrational beliefs: apply this technique to yourself. You too can engage in the exercises described in chapter 6.

5. Learn vicariously through films and biographies. You'll experience what others went through under similar circumstances.

6. Stop your negative self-talk. Negative self-talk will do nothing except bring about more self-doubt and anxiety. This, possibly more than anything else, will keep you stuck in the victim role. You'll hear all kinds of internal messages; pay attention to the ones that are supportive. If you need to snap a rubber band, on your wrist to stop your own self-disparaging remarks, just do it.

7. Take good care of yourself. You might want to lay off stimulants like caffeine and nicotine. Try to make your mealtimes a source of pleasure. Develop your own aerobic exercise program like the one you may have bugged your companion about.

8. Be sure that you have someone to talk to: a friend, counselor, or spiritual advisor.

Rebuild Your Self-Esteem

Rebuilding your self-esteem is directly related to overcoming depression. I do happen to know a few people with low self-esteem who aren't depressed, but the two states are often linked. Your self-esteem is basically the filter through which you view the world. You can see the world through a bright filter or a dark and foggy one, and the choice is up to you.

People with low self-esteem feel that they are worthless and don't have many rights. They feel they won't be listened to, so they don't take many risks. On the rare occasions when they do, they come on like gangbusters to be sure that they're heard. But the result is often the same; they feel their needs aren't acknowledged.

Victimization is connected to self-esteem in that it's couched in feelings of worthlessness. So how can you confront these crummy feelings? The crucial activity is to develop a much better mental filter that can allow you to evaluate yourself more accurately. Start by try-ing to determine if you felt low self-esteem before you began the caregiving process. If you've had feelings that you are worthless for most of your life, your poor self-esteem is characterological, that is, it's related to your character or your basic sense of identity. Cor-recting this kind of low self-esteem may take time. Many books are available to help you confront your negative self-esteem. You'll find that many means of overcoming low self-esteem are similar to those suggested for overcoming depression.

If your low self-esteem is related to your caregiving, you proba-bly need to counter your *internal critic,* the private voice that is unwilling to credit you for your efforts. Your internal critic probably uses distorted thoughts and irrational beliefs to assess your care-giving. Stop listening. Confront the critic by consciously creating better evaluations of your work, crediting yourself for your care-giving work itself as well as the outcome.

I give such advice to clients who I assist with job-seeking. Sure, they want to find work, but they're also learning a great deal about the job search itself. They need to give themselves credit for partici-pating in the process. In the future, they will always know how to look for a job. Similarly, if they develop an expertise in the process, they will have the skills to do this task forever. If your companion relapses months from now, you too will be prepared because you've come to understand the process of caring for an agoraphobe.

Examine Your Feelings of Guilt

Some joke that guilt is the "gift that keeps on giving." Others have called it a "useless emotion" that ought to be gotten rid of. But the phenomenon called *survivor guilt* exists, and you may be contending with it. If your companion is a family member, you might ask, "Why her and not me?"

As a caregiver, a better question to ask yourself is whether you're doing the work you are because of guilt or because you truly want to help your companion recover. If you are helping because you feel too guilty to not participate, you're probably adding to your feeling of victimization. If your motives are exclusively guilt-related, you'll have a hard time of it. You probably do what you do for a whole mix of reasons, though—including, yes, some guilt. The more you can deal with your guilt feelings, the more effective you'll be as a caregiver. You'll also be happier.

Two Types of Caregiving Guilt

Aside from survivor guilt, most of the guilt you will experience as a caregiver will have two sources. The first relates to how much or how little you're willing to do. Maybe you don't want to read as much as you think you should or participate in a full range of caregiving activities. Perhaps you haven't been willing to travel to your companion's therapist. When you make a decision to not contribute, that is your right. Still you may feel guilty about your decision.

The second type of guilt is related to the possibility that you've done something wrong in the caregiving process. Maybe you believe that you have played a role in making your companion more dependent on you and unwilling to recover. Or, you may have been helping your companion practice a desensitization strategy that went awry, and you blame yourself.

Most guilt feelings evolve from your assessment of yourself as in some way being bad: you're bad for not helping enough; you're bad for not reading up enough on the practice exercises; and so on So take a look at how you're assessing yourself. Confront the first type of guilt by looking at your capacity to manage your time and your life and then deciding what you can do.

Some parents alleviate their sense of guilt about not spending enough time with their kids by differentiating qualitative time from quantitative time. They do this in an effort to give time to their children when they are not feeling rushed. If that's the decision that you made with regard to caregiving, then accept it as your decision. You can say to yourself, "I looked at my time and my commitments, and this is what I know I can provide in a good-natured, productive manner." That's that.

The second type of guilt needs to be handled differently. If you've made an error in your work, or some activity hasn't panned out as you expected, you don't need to castigate yourself. If you do, you are really setting yourself up to believe that you are essentially bad. To confront this type of guilt, the first task is to get rid of three blanket distortions: should, would, and could, as in "I should do this," "I would do that if I had the time," and "I could have been more effective." Actually, by not using the word "should" you'll go quite a distance toward ending your guilt and victimization. "Should" is the language of guilt. But refraining from using all three of these words will keep your thinking from becoming too distorted.

Try also not to take any poor outcomes personally. Just because a particular exercise didn't work out doesn't mean that it's your fault or that you're responsible for the outcome. You're only half of the caregiving relationship. Don't ever lose sight of that.

Furthermore, you're in a learning process. You'll make mistakes, so learn from them. When you feel guilty about an error, then you've detracted from the learning. You and your companion will lose some of the benefits.

Finally, if you find that you need to berate yourself or you just can't go on, then try this. Put a time limit on your self-blaming, or blame yourself in a special room in your home. Then, if you need to feel guilt, feel all you want for the time that is remaining, or as long as you remain in the "guilt room." Be aware that feeling guilty takes time away from your other activities, including being there for your companion—or doing something that gives you pleasure.

Don't Ignore Your Physical Health Concerns

If you don't look and act like a victim, then you won't be one. That's a truism. I once was on a baseball team that was truly awful. I'm sure the coach had nightmares as the season approached. But he was rarely critical of our play. Instead, he told us to stay in shape in order to stay free from injuries, and to have fun. Then he added, "All of my teams look like they belong on the field." He wanted us to have a professional appearance, even if we lacked skills. As inept as we were, to this day I recall feeling proud of the team because we looked so sporty and handsome in our uniforms. He was right. We only won a few games, but we never felt victimized.

So take care of yourself. Dress well. Stay active in your companionship work. Exercise regularly. You'll actually find that your feelings of worthlessness, self-doubt, anger, and anxiety all seem to become less influential when you keep your body healthy. If you can, try to exercise with your companion. You can begin in the house and, after some practice, move the activities out of doors. If you do it with your companion, you've really accomplished two tasks at once.

Try to sleep well. Good rest will keep your caregiving energy available. During sleep, your immune system renews itself. A lack of sleep can render your immune system less effective and also make you more impulsive and irritable. At a minimum, try to make a regular period of quiet and downtime during the day. Progressive muscle relaxation can be a useful tool.

Try to watch what both you and your companion are eating. *Stealth Health* by Evelyn Tribole (1998) is an excellent resource for new ideas about your diet and feeling healthy.

Finally, try to keep some humor in your life. You can be a joy to be around. In fact, try to be the person your dog thinks you are.

Codependency

There is no shame in questioning whether or not you suffer from codependency. Beattie (1987; 1989) defined a *codependent* as "a person who has let someone else's behavior affect him or her and is obsessed with controlling other people's behavior."

Determining the degree to which you believe that you're codependent will take some exploring. You might begin by looking at how much you feel that you need to have approval or attention from others. If you need a lot of approval, you may ask yourself whether you're engaging in caregiving to receive the approval of your companion, your other family members, or your friends.

What about your own loneliness? Were you lonely before you got into the caregiving role? Do you feel that this role has given you a new lease on life? Is your companion creating a new meaning and life identity for you? That could be a problem for both of you.

People who are codependent often feel that they're not lovable and don't deserve to have any happiness. They're also prone to believe that they won't really amount to much in their lives. Before you became a caregiver, were you able to give opinions freely to others? Or did you find that you had a tendency to disparage your own ideas in favor of someone else's? Were you forever seeking approval?

Try to determine how far you go to obtain the support or the nurturance of other people. For example, though it's true that you probably became a caregiver without knowing the demands, you may stay with an activity even though it makes what you consider to be unreasonable demands of you and your time. If you find that you are often in situations like this, you may be in a pattern that could be termed codependent.

Codependency Checklist

To help determine whether or not you may engage in codependent behavior, try this checklist, which I adapted from some of Beattie's ideas.

_____ I can accept the situation I'm in.

_____ I'm able to be realistic about what I can control.

_____ I'm able to detach myself from the needs of my companion.

_____ I find that I'm able to deal with my own feelings.

_____ I take my own needs very seriously.

_____ I'm able to choose what's best for me.

_____ I'm able to set boundaries with others.

_____ I can set boundaries with my companion.

_____ I have my own life goals.

_____ I'm able to work with my companion to set goals for recovery.

_____ I can let go of problems I can't control.

_____ I'm able to relinquish helping my companion when we can't work together

_____ It's permissible for me to have feelings.

_____ I have my own problems and that's okay.

_____ I have a right to have fun in my life

_____ I am a lovable human being.

_____ I can be a great caregiver.

_____ If my companion goes berserk, it's not my fault.

_____ I have a right to my own routine.

_____ I can choose the activities I want to participate in.

_____ I can let go of worry and obsessing.

_____ I can free myself from shame and guilt.

How many of these phrases did you check off for yourself? If you had less than thirteen or fourteen, then you may need to address your codependency.

If you're codependent, you're almost certainly neglecting yourself. Furthermore, you even lose your energy for helping because your internal resources are depleted due to this self-neglect. You're assuming too much responsibility for the work with your companion, and it's not helping either of you.

Now how on earth can you be the best coach, best companion, and best caregiver you can be and still be independent, not codependent? That's a great question, and it's one that my students who are in training to become counselors ask regularly. Counselors and caregivers can't really afford to feel as if they need to be reassured by others. This often means they need to do some serious work on their own feelings of worthwhileness and self-esteem.

As a caregiver, you need to be able to make decisions independently without the advice and approval of other people. You need to be able to handle disagreements with your companion or family members and still feel that you have a lot to contribute. If you are able to function as an independent thinker, you will be better able to prevent codependency.

So, what can you do if you're codependent? Recovery from codependency can be a long-term proposition. It will involve building your own self confidence, learning to be more assertive, and learning to be in equal relationships rather than latching onto people whom you perceive as either stronger or weaker than you. You may need the help of a therapist, a support group, or a good book (I recommend Beattie's two books) to learn those new skills. Be patient with yourself.

If you've been in a codependent relationship with your companion or the family of your companion, you probably haven't felt comfortable being direct and honest. You may feel that expressing yourself will create stormy seas that can rock the lifeboat. It can be hard to give up this position of seeming safety; it can also be incredibly empowering and transformative when you finally do it.

Don't be afraid to kick the codependency habit—to go from being a cheerleader to being a leader. Your efforts will pay off in keeping you and your companion out of the codependent cycle.

Furthermore, you'll find that you'll thrive on your own decision-making capacities. You won't be afraid to articulate the solutions to the problems that your see. You will become the kind of person you want to be in your own right.

Epilogue

Your caregiving experience is yours and yours alone. You can make it pleasant, or not. You can decide to view it as an opportunity for personal reflection and change, or not. That's up to you. Just know that in my experience with all kinds of caregivers, I have seen many who were uplifted by the experience. They discovered in the role a chance for new personal discovery and life change. You, too, can choose not to be burdened and depressed by the experience. You can be mindful of the contribution you're making to yourself and another person who is significant to you. You can find inner satisfaction, peace, knowledge, and power through this role. This journey has the potential to change your life very much for the better.

Additional Help

Web Sites That Work

www.aabt.org This site is the home page of the Association for Advancement of Behavior Therapy (AABT). It provides public information about behavior therapy and cognitive behavior therapy (CBT).

www.aapb.org The home page for the Association for Applied Psychophysiology and Biofeedback is a fine repository of information about the applications of biofeedback, with an abundance of links to information sources and practioners.

www.adaa.org The site for the Anxiety Disorders Association of America is a repository of information on different fears, anxieties, and phobias. It also provides information on mental health professionals who treat anxiety disorders. The site includes a list of self-help groups as well.

www.acsm.org This is the site for the American College of Sports Medicine (ACSM) online, with information on maintaining fitness for you and your companion.

www.amtamassage.org This is the American Massage Therapy Associations (AMTA) home page. It provides detailed information about massage and massage therapy and has a national finder's service that can help you and your companion find an appropriate massage therapist. You might also check out massage training programs: Some low cost massages may be available when students are in need of subjects for training purposes.

www.anxietycoach.com. This Web site is very thoughtfully put together and is one I recommend to clients and students. It has excellent summarizing information, and is practical and easy to understand. In addition, it provides a free online newsletter.

www.anxietysupport.org This site, for ABIL, Inc. (Agoraphobics Building Independent Lives) provides information on agoraphobia and extends a national network of support groups.

www.apa.org This is the Web site for the American Psychological Association. It provides public information on mental disorders and excerpts from publications of the association.

www. dr-bob.org/tips. This popular Web site is titled the Psychopharmacology Tips Page. It provides up-to-date information based upon the clinical experiences of the contributors, so it is not a researched-based site. But the information is terrific and easy for lay people to understand.

www.encourageconnection.com This site has a host of information and inspirational ideas, including a very useful set of guidelines for helping the recovering agoraphobic in your life. Their newsletter is compiled from a great variety of different resources and offers fresh ideas and support materials.

www.familycareamerica.com This site notes that 54 million Americans suffer from some sort of disability that keeps them from going through life unaided. The site provides an array of resources and brings caregivers together interactively for mutual support, solution sharing, and discussion forums. It does cover all sorts of caregiving issues, so you may need to wade through some of the material to get to information about panic attacks and agoraphobia.

www.freedomfromfear.org This site sponsors the National Anxiety Disorders Screening Day (NADSD), an educational campaign that encourages people who suffer from anxiety and depressive illness to seek treatment. You can reach them at Freedom From Fear, 308 Seaview Ave., Staten Island, NY 10305. Their toll-free referral network number is 888-442-2022.

www.nami.org The site of the National Alliance for the Mentally Ill contains fine contributions from family members who provide caregiving services. It's also useful for finding self-help groups in your area. The organization's phone number is 800-950-6264.

www.nimh.nih.gov NIMH is the National Institute of Mental Health. You can find free information on a variety of different anxiety disorders on this site, or send for fact sheets by writing to NIMH Public Inquiries, 6001 Executive Blvd., Room 8184 MSC 9663, Bethesda, MD 20892-9663. Reach them by phone at 800-421-4211.

www.nmha.org This is the Web site for the National Mental Health Association. They can also be reached at 800-969-6642.

www.psyweb.com This site provides excellent, up-to-date information on all sorts of psychological disorders, but is particularly effective with both the panic disorders and agoraphobia with and without a history of panic disorder. The information on both psychotherapeutic treatments and pharmacotherapy is excellent, and is updated regularly. Good information is provided on normal dosage ranges as well as disorder-specific dosage ranges.

www.surgeongeneral.gov/library/mentalhealth/chapter4/sec2.html Chapter 4 of *Mental Health: A Report of the Surgeon General* offers information on mental health in adulthood, stressful life events, and the prevention of mental disorders. There is detailed information on anxiety disorders, including panic disorder and agoraphobia, and on mood disorders and schizophrenia. The site also has a variety of useful links.

www.tm.org This is the home page for Transcendental Meditation (TM), with a listing of schools and teachers.

www.touchstarpro.com For information on the creative use of different relaxation techniques, this site can be enormously useful. A variety of resources are available, including how to use humor to relax.

www.usaweekend.com Type "facing you fear" into the search field on this site for advice on how to approach a spouse or a friend who may have an anxiety disorder. You will find Mary Ellin Lerner's article, which is referred to in this book, as well as tips on how to help an anxious child.

Film Portrayals of Agoraphobics and Caregivers

Finding Forrester. 2000. Directed by Gus Van Sant.
Sean Connery plays a Pulitzer prize–winning agoraphobic novelist called William Forrester who hasn't been able to write a second novel for forty years. Ron Brown portrays high school student Jamal Wallace, a gifted student and athlete who is mentored in his writing

by the crusty Forrester. The film sensitively depicts the loneliness of agoraphobia and the positive impact that a friendship can have.

Inside Out. 1987. Directed by Robert Traicher.
Elliott Gould plays Jimmy Morgan, a once successful New York businessman who has not been able to leave his house for ten years or so. He exercises by riding a stationary bicycle while watching different videotapes of various adventure tours. He has food delivered to his door, and has sexual encounters with prostitutes who come to his apartment. Some may feel that this portrayal is a distorted picture of agoraphobia. Still, it can be useful for family members and companions to view when they need some validation of the positive impact they're having on their companion's life. The film shows the alternative, a situation where there is no caregiving.

Marvin's Room. 1996. Directed by Jerry Zaks.
This drama gives a fine portrayal of the impact of chronic illness on both the caregiver and the family.

Passion Fish. 1992. Directed by John Sayles.
Exploring the relationship between a paraplegic former daytime soap star (Mary Alice, played by Mary McDonnell) and her caregiver (Chantelle, played by Alfre Woodard), this film is not about agoraphobia, but it does address the issues that can occur in the caregiving relationship. The film also illustrates how the caregiving relationship evolves over time.

References

Abramson, L. Y., M. E. P. Seligman, and J. D. Teasdale. 1987. Learned helplessness in humans: Critique and reformulation. *Journal of Abnormal Psychology* 87:49–74.

Ackerman, D. 1999. *Deep Play.* New York: Random House.

American Psychiatric Association. 2000. *Diagnostic and Statistical Manual of Mental Disorders, Fourth Edition, Text Revision.* Washington, D.C.: American Psychiatric Association.

Aron, E. 1997. *The Highly Sensitive Person: How to Thrive When the World Overwhelms You.* New York: Broadwat Books.

Bandura, A., and R. H. Walters. 1963. *Social Learning and Personality Development.* New York: Holt, Rinehart & Winston.

Barlow, D. H. 1988. *Anxiety and Its Disorders: The Nature and Treatment of Anxiety and Panic.* New York: Guilford Press.

Barlow, D. H., and M. G. Craske. 1994. *Mastery of Your Anxiety and Panic II.* San Antonio, Tex.: Graywind Publications/The Psychological Corporation.

———. 2000. *Mastery of Your Anxiety and Panic, Client Workbook.* San Antonio, Tex.: Graywind Publications/The Psychological Corporation.

Beattie, M. 1987. *Codependent No More.* San Francisco: Harper/Hazelden.

————. 1989. *Beyond Codependency*. San Francisco: Harper/ Hazelden.

Beck, A. T. 1987. Cognitive models of depression. *Journal of Cognitive Psychotherapy: An International Quarterly* 1:5–37.

Benson, H. 1975. *The Relaxation Response*. New York: Morrow.

————. 1985. *Beyond the Relaxation Response*. New York: Berkley Books.

Blonna, R. 2000. *Coping with Stress in a Changing World*. Boston: McGraw-Hill.

Bourne, E. J. 2000. *The Anxiety and Phobia Workbook*. 3rd ed. Oakland, Calif.: New Harbinger Publications.

Bradley, L. 2000. *Manic Depression: How to Live While Loving a Manic Depressive*. Houston: Emerald Ink Publishing.

Chope, R. C. 2000. *Dancing Naked: Breaking Through the Emotional Limits That Keep You from the Job You Want*. Oakland, Calif.: New Harbinger Publications.

Cousins, N. 1979. *Anatomy of an Illness as Perceived by the Patient*. New York: Norton.

DSM-IV-TR. (See American Psychiatric Association.)

Ellis, A. 1995. Changing rational-emotive therapy (RET) to rational emotive behavior therapy (REBT). *Journal of Rational-Emotive and Cognitive Behavior Therapy* 13:85–89.

Erikson, E. H. 1950. *Childhood and Society*. New York: W. W. Norton.

Fanning, P. 1988. *Visualization for Change*. Oakland, Calif.: New Harbinger Publications.

Hadley, J., and C. Staudacher. 1996. *Hypnosis for Change*. Oakland, Calif.: New Harbinger Publications.

Hallowell, E. M. 1997. *Worry*. New York: Ballantine Books.

Hardy, A. 1976. *Agoraphobia: Symptoms, Causes and Treatment*. Menlo Park, Calif.: TSC Corporation.

Holmes, T. H., and R. H. Rahe. 1967. The social readjustment rating scale. *Journal of Psychosomatic Reasearch* 11:213–218.

Horner, A. 1986. *Being and Loving*. Northvale, N.J.: Jason Aronson.

Jacobson, E. 1970. *You Must Relax*. New York: McGraw-Hill.

Kegan, R. 1994. *In Over Our Heads: The Mental Demands of Modern Life*. Cambridge, Mass.: Harvard University Press.

Kessler, R. C., K. A. McGonagle, S. Zhao, et al. 1994. Lifetime and 12-month prevalence rates of DSM-III-R psychiatric disorders in the United States: Results from the National Comorbidity Survey. *Archives of General Psychiatry* 51:8–19

Krieger, D. 1979. *The Therapeutic Touch: How to Use Your Hands to Help or Heal.* Englewood Cliffs, N.J.: Prentice Hall.

Lazarus, A. A. 1997. *Brief but Comprehensive Psychotherapy: The Multimodal Way.* New York: Springer.

Lerner, M. E. 2000. Facing your fear. *USA Weekend,* Sept. 29–Oct. 1:8–11.

Marks, I. M. 1970. Agoraphobic syndrome (phobic anxiety state). *Archives of General Psychiatry* 23:538–553.

Meichenbaum, D. H. 1985. *Stress Innoculation Training.* New York: Pergamon.

Melamed, B. G., and L. J. Siegel. 1975. Reduction of anxiety in children facing hospitalization and surgery by use of filmed modeling. *Journal of Consulting and Clinical Psychology* 43:511-521.

McGlynn, F. D. 1994. Simple phobia. In *Handbook of Prescriptive Treatments for Adults,* edited by M. Hersen and R. T. Ammerman. New York: Plenum.

Miller, N. E. 1948. Studies of fear as an acquirable drive: I. Fear as motivation and fear-reduction as reinforcement in the learning of new responses. *Journal of Experimental Psychology* 38:89–101.

Morris, F. 1975. *Self Hypnosis in Two Days.* New York: Dutton.

———. 1979. *Hypnosis with Friends and Lovers.* New York: Harper & Row.

National Institute of Mental Health. 1993. *Understanding Panic Disorder: NIH Publication 93-3509.* Rockville, Md.: NIMH.

North, M., S. North, and J. Coble. 1996. *Virtual Reality Therapy: An Innovative Program.* Colorado Springs, Colo.: IPI Press.

Pressman, A. H. 1998. *St. John's Wort: The Miracle Medicine.* New York: Dell.

Richman, Linda. 2001. *I'd Rather Laugh: How to Be Happy Even When Life Has Other Plans for You.* New York: Warner.

Rothbaum, B. O., L. F. Hodges, R. Kooper, et al. 1995a. The efficacy of virtual reality graded exposure in the treatment of acrophobia. *American Journal of Psychiatry* 152:626–628.

————. 1995b. Virtual reality graded exposure in the treatment of ac-rophobia: A case report. *Behavior Therapy* 26:547–554.

Schachter, S. 1966. The interaction of cognitive and physiological de-terminants of the emotional state. In *Anxiety and Behavior*, edited by C. D. Spielberger. New York: Academic Press.

Schultz, J., and W. Luthe. 1959. *Autogenic Training: A Psycho-physiological Approach to Psychotherapy.* New York: Grune & Stratton.

Seligman, M. E. P. 1974. Depression and learned helplessness. In *The Psychology of Depresiion: Contemporary Theory and Research,* edited by R. J. Friedman and M. M. Katz. Washington, D.C.: Winston-Wiley.

Seligman, M. E. P, and D. L. Rosenhan. 1998. *Abnormality.* New York: W.W. Norton.

Stampfl, T. G., and D. J. Levis. 1967. Essentials of implosive therapy: A learning-theory-based psychodynamic behavioral therapy. *Journal of Abnormal Psychology* 72:496-503.

Stroebel, C. 1978. *The Quieting Response Training: Introduction.* New York: BMA.

Strong, K. V. 1997. *Anxiety, Panic Attacks and Agoraphobia—Informa-tion for Support People, Family and Friends.* 2nd ed. Vancouver Is-land, Canada: Oakminster Publishing.

Suinn, R., and F. Richardson. 1971. Anxiety management training: A non-specific behavior therapy program for anxiety control. *Be-havior Therapy* 2:498–512.

Tribole, E. 1998. *Stealth Health.* New York: Viking/Penguin.

Wallace, R. K. 1970. The physiological effects of trancendental medi-tation. *Science* 167:1751–1754.

Williams, K. P. 1993 . *How to Help Your Loved One Recover from Agora-phobia.* Far Hills, N.J.: New Horizon Press.

Wolpe, J. 1958. *Psychotherapy by Reciprocal Inhibition.* Stanford, Calif.: Stanford University Press.

Wolpe, J., and D. Wolpe. 1988. *Life without Fear.* Oakland, Calif.: New Harbinger Publications.

Zuercher-White, E. 1998. *An End to Panic: Breakthrough Techniques for Overcoming Panic Disorder.* 2nd ed. Oakland, Calif.: New Harbin-ger Publications.

Robert Chope, Ph.D., is a professor of counseling at San Francisco State University and a psychologist in private practice who has been working with agoraphobics and their families for more than twenty years. He is the author of *Dancing Naked: Breaking Through the Emotional Limits that Keep You from the Job You Want.*

Some Other
New Harbinger Titles

The Anxiety & Phobia Workbook, 3rd edition, Item PHO3 $19.95

Beyond Anxiety & Phobia, Item BYAP $19.95

The Self-Nourishment Companion, Item SNC $10.95

The Healing Sorrow Workbook, Item HSW $17.95

The Daily Relaxer, Item DALY $12.95

Stop Controlling Me!, Item SCM $13.95

Lift Your Mood Now, Item LYMN $12.95

An End to Panic, 2nd edition, Item END2 $19.95

Serenity to Go, Item STG $12.95

The Depression Workbook, Item DEP $19.95

The OCD Workbook, Item OCD $18.95

The Anger Control Workbook, Item ACWB $17.95

Flying without Fear, Item FLY $14.95

The Shyness & Social Anxiety Workbook, Item SHYW $15.95

The Relaxation & Stress Reduction Workbook, 5th edition, Item RS5 $19.95

Energy Tapping, Item ETAP $14.95

Stop Walking on Eggshells, Item WOE $14.95

Angry All the Time, Item ALL 12.95

Living without Procrastination, Item $12.95

Hypnosis for Change, 3rd edition, Item HYP3 $16.95

Don't Take it Personally, Item DOTA $15.95

Toxic Coworkers, Item TOXC $13.95

Letting Go of Anger, Item LET $13.95

Call **toll free, 1-800-748-6273,** or log on to our online bookstore at **www.newharbinger.com** to order. Have your Visa or Mastercard number ready. Or send a check for the titles you want to New Harbinger Publications, Inc., 5674 Shattuck Ave., Oakland, CA 94609. Include $4.50 for the first book and 75¢ for each additional book, to cover shipping and handling. (California residents please include appropriate sales tax.) Allow two to five weeks for delivery.

Prices subject to change without notice.